50 YEARS OF HARD ROAD

A Vagrant's Journey

NICK CHARLES MBE

HAWKSMOOR
PUBLISHING

First published 2021 by Hawksmoor Publishing

Kemp House, 152-160 City Rd, London, EC1V 2NX

www.hawksmoorpublishing.com

ISBN: 9781914066054 [Hardback] | 9781914066122 [Softback]

Nick Charles has asserted his right under the Copyright, Designs and Patents Act, 1988 to be identified as the author of this book.

Copyright 2021. All Rights Reserved. No part of this publication may be reproduced, stored in a retrieval system, or transmitted in any form or by any means, electronic, mechanical, photocopying, recording or otherwise, without the prior permission of the publisher.

A CIP catalogue record for this book is available from the British Library.

This book is sold subject to the condition that it shall not, by way of trade or otherwise, be lent, re-sold, hired out or otherwise circulated without the publisher's prior consent in any form of binding or cover other than that in which it is published and without a similar condition including this condition being imposed on the subsequent purchaser.

Picture Credits

Image 1 – reproduced with the kind permission of Marketa Luskacova. ©Marketa Luskacova.

FOREWORD

I have worked with Nick Charles for the best part of 40 years and have never come across anyone with such unending passion and commitment to his vocation. He has lived as an alcoholic, both drunk and sober, for 45 years and is a supreme expert in his field. I have enormous respect for his knowledge, expertise and fightback from the depths of despair, following the destruction that he suffered.

From the very first day I met him, I was struck by his 'all or nothing' approach to absolutely every aspect of his life. Some can find this a little overpowering, but I firmly believe that without it, he would never have achieved in the way he has.

This is a man who stopped drinking two days before his birthday, two weeks before Christmas and spent an agonising detox working behind the bar of a busy London pub, serving others with the very thing his body and brain were screaming out for. This pretty much gives you the measure of the man. No surprise then that he went on to set up and establish the biggest and most successful residential rehab unit in the country at the time, the Chaucer Clinic. Many years later, he adapted his teachings to be used in an outreach setting across Cambridgeshire with the Gainsborough Foundation, in partnership with 150+ GPs. His valuable work was recognised when he received the MBE *'for services to people with alcohol problems'*, and together with the awards that followed during his GP outreach service, his work became the most decorated in the UK alcohol treatment field.

Working alongside him has been remarkable, frustrating, hilarious, humbling, crazy, educational, creative, sad, emotional, infuriating and inspirational in equal measures of experience… but it has never been dull! I have rubbed shoulders along the way with major celebrities of the entertainment and media world, some of whom were treated by Nick and others who supported his work financially. There have also been eminent professors, medical consultants, psychiatrists and politicians along with homeless street drinkers, criminals, and victims of others' cruelty, neglect, abuse and violence.

All of Nick's entrepreneurial ventures, and there are far too many to write about here, have funded his alcohol treatment work at their core, and all were given the same application and unending belief in success, no matter what they were. I first went to work with Nick as a keyboard backing musician for him and his wife, the TV and film actress Lesley Roach, who were a very successful cabaret duo. This led to running an agency supplying hundreds of managed pubs across London and the Home Counties, with good class self-contained entertainers. Our company was then contracted to provide PR and marketing services for touring theatrical productions, including those of Andrew Lloyd Webber and John Gale – this was a wonderful fun time, and I met and worked with many well-known personalities and great actors. One, Andrew Sachs, became a close friend to us all.

All of the profits went to support Nick's work through day centres and busy helplines, so he was able to continue helping those who needed him the most. My role by now was running the administration and business management for all his projects.

In 1989, Dr David Marjot, the Regional Consultant Psychiatrist for Addiction with North West Thames Health Authority, and also a keen supporter and colleague of Nick's work, secured us disused wards on a large psychiatric hospital estate. Chaucer Clinic was a dream turned into reality, albeit a hugely challenging one for us all. Dr Marjot later became Consultant Adviser to the clinic and subsequently for Nick's further projects, and has remained in this role to the present day. It was here that Nick's teachings began to be shaped into the structured, multi-award winning, educational, recovery programme now known as 'ANSWERS' which will soon be available online.

Nick has never given up on a patient, and has aided the recovery of many who others had written off. I have watched people go on to lead fulfilling lives, attain qualifications, embark on successful careers, get married, have children and travel the world. In short, anything seemed to become possible for those who did it Nick's way, alcohol-free with a smile and happy heart. He describes himself as a salesman; he sells sobriety to those who would prefer to spend their money on a drink. I have witnessed such successes first-hand, over and over again.

In the early days, I mistook his vision as a man simply blinded by obsession; his ambition and determination as misplaced at best, and deluded at worst. But his message of hope and achievement has saved an incalculable number of lives. I truly believe that one of the reasons his recovery programme has been so hugely successful is that it has been written and delivered by someone with personal experience and empathy. Together with Nikki de Villiers, who has also suffered terribly, and the only person I have met who shares Nick's enthusiasm, they have an unrivalled success rate of recovery, sustained over decades. Alcohol dependency and addiction is a difficult illness to comprehend for those who have not suffered from it, and their insight is paramount to meaningful treatment. Supported by his wife, Lesley, who has been beside Nick for almost all of his sober life, and my own business management skills, 'ANSWERS' has paved the way to recovery for many victims, often sparing them the depths of desperation that Nick endured.

50 Years of Hard Road is a unique adventure story. It is a compilation of biographical, historical life journey data – hard-hitting but containing vital lessons, with succinct and meaningful one-line messages. This combined with a personal and reflective account of how Nick fought his way back from the brink, to compile a unique treatment programme.

I feel proud to have played a part in what I can only describe as an odyssey, and knowing Nick as well as I do, I am confident he will continue to help those who most need him… for as long as he has breath in his body.

Teresa Weiler, Project Manager Chaucer Clinic/Gainsborough Foundation and PA to Nick Charles MBE for 38 years.

INTRODUCTION

Welcome to the *Inner World* of the totally addicted alcohol dependent. I believe a conducted tour of this place, described through the eyes and twisted psyche of a victim of total alcohol addiction, is vital. It will help the reader understand the shift in the wiring of a complex psychiatric system. This will bring about a better understanding of the forthcoming events.

It is extremely difficult to explain to someone who has no knowledge or understanding of alcohol addiction, the deep sensation of comfort, confidence, and well-being experienced between the addict and their drink. That those recovering can often be heard to refer to their drinking days as, '*My affair with Madam Alcohol*' or '*I know we were incompatible, but I so miss my best friend*' is an indication of the intensity of the experience.

For some, the feeling to remain within the *Inner World* for as long as possible is so overwhelming it is impossible to resist – enter the world of total alcohol dependency.

But first, let us attempt to describe the *Inner World*. Try to imagine a fantasy where you become King or Queen; where you are the centre of attention and are in complete control of your destiny. Imagine that, like James Bond, you flirt with danger yet always come out on top and return the victor, complete with adulation and credit. Consider a place where you are hailed most popular, most desirable, and indestructible. There you have that *Inner World,* which is the favourite living place of the alcohol dependent.

During my career, I have met many of those addicted to alcohol, their loved ones, and those-near-and-dear to them, who are not only unable to understand the mystery of alcohol's effect, but are completely baffled by it. They must not despair; the vast majority of the human race, led by the medical profession, are equally at a loss. However, for the reader of '*50 Years of Hard Road*' to understand the insanity – and alcohol addiction is indeed a form of insanity – it is important for me to explain, and fill in some of the grey areas.

Firstly, allow me to establish that alcohol dependents are like fingerprints, they are all the same until you look closely, and then you see the differences. This is because everyone has a different degree of resistance to alcohol, and together with variations in personalities, this means each is unique. The best example I can offer to describe the difficulties every dependant wishing to stop has to face, came about one day in a telephone call from my long-time agent and dear friend, the late Kenneth Earle.

It was early in the year 2002, and the influential Kenneth had received an anguished call from an associate, who was connected to the actor Sir Anthony Hopkins. The call revealed that in an interview, Sir Anthony had said, "Being addicted to alcohol has been an amazing and powerful experience I wouldn't have missed for the world."

There followed a battery of abuse from members of the public, and the phone call was to ask if I would be prepared to explain, via a letter to the press, precisely what Anthony had meant. In no way had there been any intention to glorify the experience. It appeared Kenneth's associate thought that I would be better disposed to undertake the task than anyone else; would I write a letter to a national newspaper and attempt to put things right? I admired Sir Anthony Hopkins hugely, and he was the only person I knew who had been alcohol-free longer than I had, and by almost a year. I agreed at once.

I hoped my letter, which was published in the Daily Mail on Wednesday, March 6th 2002, would go some way to help the reader understand the enormous task facing the alcohol dependent, prior to their last drink.

Sir Anthony was attempting the almost impossible – to describe the battle he had faced in order to break free of alcohol, how it had such a grip on him, and why it was such a monumental task. Here is a condensed version of the letter.

'To beat Alcoholism and attain sobriety means a permanent process of unlearning all of the arrogance, deceit, conceit, illusion, delusion and dishonesty that, through alcohol, we have been training ourselves into for years. It means killing a part of ourselves and undergoing a kind of death – but there is an enormous reward. A fully recovered alcoholic will gain a unique insight into life and human nature, a quality to a degree never found

in someone who hasn't had the experience. It's a mixture of wisdom and humility, manifesting itself in a feel for life and its mysteries similar, perhaps, to a God-given gift possessed by a master orator, poet or philosopher. Once recovered, we've undergone a metamorphosis which has given us an added reverence and greater profundity – Closer to God, in fact.'

Sir Anthony was absolutely right... I wouldn't have missed it either!

Naturally enough, none of this helped lessen the agonies, both mental and physical, for the habitual drunk breaking free, and delusion reigns supreme. There is no awareness of the time factor for this group, only night and day with lifetimes in between. It is perhaps not widely known (or realised) that alcohol is an anaesthetic, which has been used as such on battlefields for time immemorial. All alcoholic drinks contain ethyl alcohol, a drug similar to those used in operating theatres to perform surgery. Itinerant homeless drinkers have been involuntarily anaesthetising themselves for the duration, making time infinite.

A good example of this is a friendship I struck up during my time on the streets. His name was Jeff, and one day someone commented, in a down-at-heel bar we used, that we must be joined at the hip. Whenever he saw one of us, the other was never far behind. He went on to ask how long we had been friends and there was a pause while we both reflected. I suggested it must be about a year; Jeff was adamant it was more like two. The following day I consulted the hostel reception registration book, which revealed we had met ten weeks previously. Looking back, I had many Jeff-type friendships, as many as a dozen, and it always seemed we had been friends for years after a week or so. There was never a Jeff, in reality; I cannot remember any of their names and my recollection is I called them all Jeff. None of them seemed to mind.

Another example of the anaesthetic created by alcohol is in the case of The Doc and Ginger, two pivotal figures in my recovery. The duration of the relationships from beginning to end, shocked even me when I worked out a possible timeframe for the writing of this book. They occurred somewhere between the late summer of 1975 and the early winter of 1976. They were then, and remain to this day, lifelong experiences. The Doc's influence upon my work was massive. He gave me confidence and self-belief in my addiction studies, and without this, I am sure I would not be writing this book. Yet, I cannot remember his name and have had to use a pseudonym that I know he would have understood. Ginger was equally important. She allowed me a brief window into the real world, and I am so grateful to her. When my MBE was announced in the national press, she made contact and told me how thrilled she was; she was happily married to an old school friend of hers, and they had two children.

Incredibly, one friendship did survive from those dreadful days. After my appearance on the Irish RTE Television Saturday night show '*Kenny Live*' with Pat Kenny in Dublin, I received a call from Des Casement. We had met in the Petticoat Lane Salvation Army Hostel in 1975, and we shared many memories, particularly those of The Doc. Des is a delightful man who recognised my problems and showed me much understanding. I recall once losing a pen, a precious item in those days of destitution, and Des bought me a new one as a present. We spoke recently and mused over the possibility we were the only survivors of that dreadful era. It was with heavy hearts we struggled to remember those who were now faceless and nameless, amongst the homeless, alcohol-addicted street people of days gone by.

The intensity described in my letter to the Daily Mail to aid Sir Anthony Hopkins dilemma was never more prevalent than in the cases of these friendships.

1: THE END OF THE BEGINNING

'The trouble with dying is it's so bloody final!'

I was lying flat on my back across a railway track, a hundred yards up from my local railway station with my head on the line, and spoke the words aloud to no one. It wasn't that I was having second thoughts, but the insanity which ruled my every living moment reminded me my favourite football team had a game coming up, and I would never get to know the result!

I'd planned the exit from my troubled world with little precision; indeed, there was only one essential detail, a flask-shaped bottle of brandy. I reached for it hurriedly from an inside pocket before my guardian angel – always assuming I had one – had time to step in and stop me. It took no time at all to empty the contents, and I fought my body's natural reaction to throw it back up, and then made myself as comfortable as I could with my head resting on the cold steel.

It was almost dark or maybe nearly light, time and tide were lost on me, but it was during the minutes when the planet gives the impression it doesn't know what to do next. I had no idea it was autumn 1974. Normal folk know these things, of course. They have people to see, places to go, stuff to do; in their lives, it matters if it's day or night. Time meant nothing to me, it was inconsequential and only offered more pain, more trial and tribulation, and the additional complication of working out where my next drink was coming from. Food didn't present a problem as there were always waste bins, and begging for coins to buy a bag of chips was easy enough, unless I smelt so vile people hurried by or crossed over the road before they reached me.

Suddenly, I realised the light was fading, it was night that was beckoning and I was happier with that, I would remain invisible to the human eye until they found me in daylight minus my head.

It was sunshine that greeted me when I opened my eyes and I couldn't move. I tried but nothing worked except the fingers on one hand, but even then hardly at all and I was unable to understand why. I could hear distant traffic and the sounds of a civilisation I had long abandoned, and put more effort into forcing my limbs into freeing myself from invisible bonds. At last, and after a supreme effort, I rolled onto one side and was violently sick. I staggered to my feet after several false starts and began a long and painful journey to the station platform a couple of hundred yards away. The railway sleepers were an almost impossible hurdle, there were many and they seemed never-ending, but finally I reached the slope leading to the deserted passenger area. I pondered momentarily about a day, long ago, when I had caught a train and travelled first class from this very place. Then, I sank onto a bench with wrought iron sides and decided I needed a drink.

I looked around me, every slight movement was agony, there was not a soul in sight and I decided it must be early and I'd got there before anyone else. When humans arrived, I would pretend I was waiting for a train; it would buy me time to think and I had plenty of that. Then, I caught sight of a large brown sign.

It had long metal legs and white letters announcing some sort of message but my eyes wouldn't focus. I tried hard without success and realised I needed to get closer. It was a mammoth struggle but I made it, and the words told me the station was closed to rail traffic. Perhaps death was not my way out!

I left through a hole in a wire netting fence and onto a hill which led to the town centre and found another bench. Slowly, my memory returned, but not all of it, and I was glad. My marriage had ended, I'd arrived back at the family home and the locks had been changed... no woman would have wanted a drunk like me for a husband. I searched what was left of my memory in an effort to reason how it had happened and why it had happened; everyone had a drink, didn't they?

In my remembrances, I was back in the school playground when I heard a voice – in the real world – say my name. 'Is that you Nick... Nick, is that you?'

I looked up, but it hurt. I cried out in pain and had to move my head back again, and then to one side, so I could look at the voice. Despite my condition, I recognised Maid Marian[1] immediately, and felt instant shame for the cowardly way I had treated her previously.

I had met Marian one day, in another life, when I found myself in the reception at the local hospital where I unexpectedly recognised the mum of one of my friends, who was a manager at the hospital. My friend's mum had welcomed me demonstratively, and we were deep in conversation when a delightfully pretty and slender young woman of around my own age approached us, apologising for the interruption. The young woman was the manager's secretary and I was left alone with her while my pal's mum went to take a phone call. Marian and I had our first date that night.

The *reason* for my cowardly act had occurred long before we met. I was in my middle teens and had a girlfriend who worked in the village where I was brought up. At her request, and in the days when women rarely went into pubs alone, I agreed to accompany a mixed-race friend of hers to a local bar so she had an excuse to be there. Once inside, I could return to my girlfriend's place of work, having completed the good turn. When I arrived home later that day, it was to find my mother in a state of utter fury. She flew at me like a wildcat accusing me of having a black girlfriend, and threatened me with a fate worse than death should I bring a black child back home. I was at a loss to understand her point of view, or how she had received such news so quickly. We'd had a black girl in my class at school, and I never ever thought of her as being different to the rest of us, or that she was anything other than a very pretty girl and a school friend.

When I started dating Marian, years later, our relationship was going well and my heart missed a beat each time I saw her, until a friend told me she was a result of a mixed-race family. The memory of my mother's attack concerning such relationships provoked a fear in me of the worst kind in those dark and different days. I offered Marian no explanation (how could I tell her, what could I say?); I simply didn't pick her up one night and never saw her again. Until now.

It was Maid Marian who stood before me, somehow recognising who I was when my own family would have probably had difficulty.

I rubbed my eyes hard and my vision cleared sufficiently to see her lovely face and two delightful children.

'Yes, it *is* me, Maid Marian,' I said, my face wet with tears which were beyond control. 'They are lovely children,' I managed nodding in their direction.

'They should have been yours,' she said in a voice I could barely hear.

'You had a narrow escape Maid Marian, believe me!' I replied. 'My family didn't deserve you and yours, and you deserved better than me and mine.' I meant every word. There was a silence which seemed to last forever, and then she spoke a little louder and with conviction, 'Whatever has happened to you would not have done so, had you belonged to me!'

'Please go, Maid Marian,' I begged, and reluctantly she did.

I can't say if I had been in love with her, but I can say quite conclusively, I am still in love with the memory of Maid Marian.

Two days later, I awoke in the county psychiatric hospital.

---

[1] Her name was indeed Marian but I added the *Maid* bit because she reminded me of the actress who played Lady Marian Fitzwalter in the popular TV series '*Robin Hood*'.

2: RECOLLECTIONS

Although I have no recollection of doing so, I had telephoned 'The Samaritans' and somehow made my way to a branch office from where I was taken to hospital for assessment. Thanks to this wonderful organisation, I was processed quickly and admitted at once.

I lay alone in a side room for the first two days of my stay, apart from the medication points conducted by an elderly nurse, and the arrival of a meals lady. I was glad because it gave me time to think. My thoughts and the events leading up to becoming homeless were scrambled, and I was attempting to make sense of what had happened to me. It was hard, not helped by the fact I was heavily medicated, which – on enquiry – I was told would prevent me from having another alcohol seizure. This puzzled me beyond words.

Confusion continued to reign supreme, compounded on the third day by being told I had to attend an AA (Alcoholics Anonymous) meeting. Once out of my side bedroom, I found myself in a large oval common room with doors at intervals around the perimeter leading to bedrooms like mine. There were coffee tables spaced out, each with comfortable chairs, and there seemed to be a pleasant atmosphere. I selected an unoccupied one, sat down, and tried to look inconspicuous.

Almost at once, a young man joined me and began to talk at speed, and I simply couldn't keep up. I had no idea what he was talking about. I picked up odd words about planetary systems and aliens, but there was nothing that made sense. Abruptly, he asked me a question that I didn't comprehend either, and after waiting for several seconds for a response, he wandered off.

The room began to fill up with other patients arriving from behind bedroom doors like mine, and soon I had three companions who joined me at my chosen table. They each said hello and told me their names. One shook my hand and I said my name back, and it pleased me that there were no questions this time. I listened to the murmur of conversation around the room until a nurse read out my name and beckoned me to follow her. She invited me to take a chair in a small office and then spoke very slowly with the first words I had understood since waking that morning.

'I'm Nurse Winterbottom… and I've heard all the jokes. The patients call me CB, and you can too if you wish,' she began. 'Nothing will be making much sense to you right now because you're on seriously strong medication,' she continued. 'You have had an alcohol seizure recently and possibly more than one in the last few weeks. Also, you are probably suffering from malnutrition. Do you understand Nick?' I nodded, surprised she used my name.

'Now, I want you to stop me if you have any questions along the way while I talk you through the treatment plan the doctors have devised for you. To begin with, you are currently going through a detoxification process. Do you know what that is?' I shook my head.

'Your body has become saturated, overwhelmed, drenched, soaked, soused if you like, by alcohol. You need to be rid of what is, in effect, a poison. You have to be cleansed. It is a purification process which has become necessary because you have become contaminated by alcohol. At the time of admission, you were in a state of collapse and in a degenerated condition physically and mentally. Detoxification or detox will rid you of the cause of this deterioration and perform the cleansing processes safely, and with the least distress to you and your system. Some people have been known to die because they go cold turkey when they cease drinking without a medically controlled detox.'

My body felt like it had been run over by a steamroller, and my head thumped in time with my heartbeat. Somehow my brain understood – through CB's words – the severity of my condition, which she had described so eloquently. Frankly, I was frightened by the diagnosis she had spelt out to me.

'I would like you to attend the hospital AA meeting which begins in about half an hour,' she said, looking at her wristwatch. 'Have you ever been to one?' I shook my head.

'Follow me.' CB stood and guided me back to the table I had recently vacated and asked another patient if they would be kind enough to accompany me to the meeting. I turned to thank her, but all I could see through blurred vision was her back in the distance.

*

The AA meeting was based on 12 religious steps and seemed to be a confessional too. Those who elected to speak did so confidently, and some appeared to take delight in their drunken antics, which they made to sound funny. I suppose they were, although I viewed them as sad and would have been ashamed to relate any of the so-called funny things that had happened to me. Nevertheless, I came away with much food for thought, although I knew instinctively this recovery device would not be for me.

As the days passed, I discovered a new personality and disposition; one I hadn't perceived since before my first alcoholic drink. My fellow inmates seemed to like what they saw in me, and I liked them too; we had a mixed bag of problems, with alcohol at the root, making up a ward of twenty patients. CB (who I discovered was a psychiatric nurse) was a great listener, and she and I had a one-to-one session each afternoon, as did some of the others. There were two other nurses, one male, who were similarly qualified, and they shared the patient load.

Along the way, CB asked me many questions, including a request to list the changes that occurred in my personality when I was drinking. She gave me an exercise book and a ballpoint pen and instructed me to spend as much time on the task as I possibly could. I was keen to please, so I set about the task at once.

I enjoyed writing and had written several pages before reading them back. When I did so, I found the contents alarming. I described how as little as a pint of beer would flick a switch and transport me into an inner world full of confidence and ambition, but it would also create unreal imaginings. I would become someone else and believe in my own new identity. I recalled concocting stories of false and fantastical events and regaling them to anyone who would listen to my insane imaginings. The truth, and anything which resembled me when sober, was lost in a maelstrom of unreality.

My drinking had long reached the stage where I consumed alcohol every day, and I had become unemployable. Then, one day, I had been hospitalised due to a motor vehicle accident and entered an enforced period of sobriety. This time, instead of awaking with shameful memories of what I had enacted while under the influence, I remained in my other world. It took the hospital and police authorities almost two weeks to determine my true identity, and a further week before my memory began to return to normality.

Looking at the pages of my notebook, I paused. I was unsure if I wanted another living soul to see my words, and then remembered some biblical advice… confession is good for the soul. I allowed CB to see my efforts, and she took them away before returning them safely.

*

After dinner, it was customary for us to sit and while away the time chatting. The conversation varied widely but was never far away from the reason we were hospitalised. That night, I retired early, having opened the bedroom window to its limit, which I felt offered a degree of freedom. I lay listening to distant music from somewhere, and the gentle hum of conversation drifted in from the common room. It felt comforting and I began to doze fitfully.

Abruptly, I was wide awake, distracted by the sound of an instrumental pop recording called 'Telstar' recorded by *The Tornados*' and produced by the legendary Joe Meek. It was the first-ever UK instrumental to top the American charts, and I had got preciously close to being part of it…

*

I had been a semi-professional vocalist and musician when I met Roger Lavern. He was a former soldier in the Household Cavalry who played keyboards in a way that, together with outrageous good looks, turned female audiences into putty.

I met him through a friend I knew from my days in the Boy Scouts. There was a senior group called the '*Rover Crew*', and Bill Cordell, a member of this troupe, sold me his guitar so he could buy an engagement ring. It was a Hofner cut-away sporting twin pick-ups and designed to be used more professionally than my cheap, hard to play pretender with a hole in the middle. I had fond memories of learning to play it, and eventually singing my first ever self-accompanied song called *'Puttin' on the Style'*.

I thought of Roger Lavern quite often and how we'd had a strange on and off friendship over many years. Momentarily, in my room, I considered the possibility of playing with him once again, and quickly dismissed it as futile and wishful thinking. Then my thoughts switched to my dalliance with suicide and I wanted rid of this line of thought too. I was trying not to dwell on death, and looked to concentrate instead on the odds of my survival and any likelihood I might have of a future.

Suddenly, I wondered if I still had a singing voice and tried to sing a line out loud. Immediately, there was a sudden rush of wings in the room and I opened my eyes wide, thinking my time had come and I was being greeted by angels. Then I relaxed; I had scared a couple of pigeons off the ledge outside my bedroom window.

'Is there anything you need, Nick?'

I switched on a safety wall light next to my pillow and it revealed the concerned face of CB doing her nightly rounds. 'I heard a noise,' she explained whilst her eyes scanned around my tiny place. 'I thought I would make sure you were okay,' she added. I blamed a dream, and as she was about to depart, I called her back. 'What does CB stand for?' I asked, realising I was beginning to think straight again. '**C**old **B**um,' replied Nurse Winterbottom with a cheeky smile on her face.

*

I had little control over my thought patterns, and as I lay in a drugged and dreamlike state, I got to thinking about the music scene and how I had got involved.

In the heady music days of the 1950s and early 1960s, and before the Beatles, Skiffle heralded the introduction to rock and roll. Its origins are obscure (that's one thing most purists seem to agree on), but without it there would have been no rock and roll, and music – as we know it today – may have developed quite differently. It is highly possible the genre originated in the African-American musical culture of the early 20th century and developed from there. It caused a sensation when introduced to the British public with a fast tempo single-disc recording called '*Rock Island Line*' in 1955, featuring Lonnie Donegan.

It had an influential but fairly short life, as is sometimes the case with musical fads and crazes; however, it made a never to be forgotten and indelible mark in modern music history. It influenced but was ultimately replaced by American sounds and some tuneful but somewhat mundane British efforts.

I was fresh out of the Boy Scouts, and my two local heroes were Bill (who, as mentioned, had sold me his Hofner guitar) and Tony Goodwin, a local heartthrob that many people tipped for stardom. They were nearby neighbours to where I lived with my parents in constabulary-owned houses adjacent to the police station; my father was a copper. Both were handsome fellows and while Bill attempted the sophisticated approach to air his showbiz wares, Tony was a rocker and actor. He had suave, gypsy good looks, and he left a trail of broken hearts behind when he married Nellie, his long-time girlfriend. He possessed multi-talented abilities, which would have taken him onto the West End Stage had he been born in a place more worldly and cultured than our local village. In the 1950s, it offered little more than rural beauty where young people could but dream.

I had brief musical liaisons with both Bill and Tony, one of which – to a twelve-year-old boy – was memorable for its adventure and sheer audacity in days of yore.

Situated fifteen or so miles away was Dudley, which while in the heart of the Black Country, was actually still in Worcestershire. It was a busy industrial town and sported a large theatre called the Dudley Hippodrome and all sorts of good quality entertainment were featured there. One evening in the middle 1950s, there was a knock on our front door which, when my mother answered, revealed Bill and Tony, whom she idolised. They asked if I was doing anything and, if not, could I help at the scout hut where they had some sorting out to do. She already had my coat in her hands when I was summoned from the lounge, and I was delighted to be needed by such heroes.

We did go to the scout hut, and they *had* been performing scouting duties, but this had all been completed by the time they came looking for me. We entered an office type room which on scout nights was the domain of the Scout Master, but tonight it belonged to us alone.

'We have a proposition for you, Nick.' My eyes opened up like saucers, and I was aware of this because I had to consciously close and open them again so as not to look awestruck.

'There's a talent competition coming up at Dudley Hip,' said Bill, abbreviating the second word in its title as many Midlanders did. 'We think you could win it.' My expression turned to astonishment, but before I could protest, Tony intervened.

'There's going to be twenty acts, three judges and three prizes. First prize is £30, second prize £20, and third prize £10. The money is being put up by a local factory owner and we think you and your choirboy voice can win something.'

'But there is a slight problem!' added Bill, who didn't look his usual confident self, and I waited nervously. 'It's a weekday variety matinee talent show, so you'll have to play truant from school.' I was horrified.

'I can't do that! How would I do that?' I felt a mixed reaction because I already wanted to go.

'There's another snag, at least you might think so.' Tony was smiling as he spoke, so I smiled back but soon wished I hadn't. 'Bill and I are going to enter too. You see, we need some more equipment for the band, and if we get lucky, we could get it with the prize money. A bloke we know has got a load of stuff he's hardly used and wants to get rid of it; he'll take £30 for the lot.'

Tony looked at me expectantly, and then Bill chimed in. 'Our reasoning is that… with the three of us going out by ourselves… there are three chances of winning something. We've also had some insider information.'

'What's that,' I asked.

Bill breathed in deeply. 'A local Dudley agent called Vic Kendrick has tipped us off that the audience will be mainly women – you know, housewives like your mother. He reckons if some angelic kid with a decent voice goes on and sings *Ave Maria*, we'll walk it, and you've got the voice. Anyway, we've got a halfway decent plan; do you want to hear it?'

I nodded.

They both shuffled; I sat stock-still. This time it was Tony.

'The show is on a Friday at 3pm, so school as usual in the morning. Your mum is in on it,' my head shot up, but Tony ploughed on. 'She will ring the school when you go home for lunch to say you have a migraine; this won't cause suspicion seeing as you've had them since you hit your head a while ago. As for your dad, he is at work, so if we're late back, she will say it's a scouting thing.'

This news made me feel easier, but I was amazed how much thought had gone into it, and even more surprised Mum had managed to keep it to herself.

'Yes,' I said.

'Yes, what?' they both asked in accidental unison.

'Yes, I'll do it,' I replied. 'But I'll have to brush up on the words.' They both sighed with relief, and I felt a rare sense of importance.

My mother's dearest wish was that I would be successful as a singer and she spent hours listening to me rehearsing in the kitchen; she was also a scrupulously honest woman and I did wonder about her willingness to let me bunk off school! When I got home, she gave me a hug and her face was wreathed in smiles. 'Just treat it as one of those solos you sing at school,' was all she said reassuringly.

*

The big day arrived and everything went according to plan, except poor Bill had a sore throat. We travelled there together, went through a booking-in process on arrival, and the atmosphere reminded me of nothing more than a big night behind the scenes at a school play. We were given a running order and I was somewhere mid-table; Bill was placed towards the end, but poor Tony was elected to open the show. Like the stoic person he was, he took it in good heart.

We were to be backed by an organist, bass and drums, and a comedian compere opened the show. Then it was show time and Tony was incredible. He sang an Al Jolson medley and brought the house down. I think it settled the nerves for all those who had them, but I was still calm and began to fear the possibility it might hit me at the last minute. I needn't have worried; I sang as I hoped I would, and the audience reaction was great. Bill did well too, and in fact, the whole show was a success. Eventually, it came to an end and it was judgement time.

In first place was a Welsh tenor who I thought was marvellous. Second was Tony, and I was delighted to be judged third. The biggest thrill was that we pooled the money and had enough money to buy the equipment for the band. I was even more pleased when he told me I could sing a number with them at their next performance, and my mum was as proud as punch. 'Never mind, my lad,' she said with more than a trace of her Black Country accent, 'Your time will come.'

Soon afterwards, and on Bill's recommendation, I joined a local four-piece group called the '*Saddle Tramps*' who were as new and inexperienced as I was. I had signed up for guitar lessons in an industrial town some four miles away, and it took this experience for me to realise just how far behind I was, having previously been pretty much self-taught. Some months later, Bill came to see me at home where I lived with my parents and asked me to sing him a couple of songs which I did. He told me I had improved beyond belief, and he knew a group called '*The Zodiacs*' who were based a few miles away and who were looking for a singer. Was I interested? Their leader was Butch Bowen, and less than a month later, we did our first booking together.

They had a pianist who rattled the keys like no one I had ever heard before in my life, his name was Roger Jackson – soon to be Roger Lavern – and I would have a love-hate musical relationship with him for the rest of his life.

Roger left '*The Zodiacs*' soon after I joined to pursue a solo career. A year later, I met him in the street and he invited me to join the '*Roger Lavern Combo*' and it gave me something to think about. Butch Bowen and I had become close friends, although this was about to change when the group had the opportunity to replace me with a star name. Butch was understandably ambitious and deep down I knew there was something missing in my rock/pop group mentality make-up. I went to see Tony to ask his advice and poured out my heart, He listened carefully, and when I finally ran out of words, he took a deep breath and said simply,

'You're an entertainer Nick, not a rock group player. Take Roger's offer. I think you will move forward with him.'

I took the advice.

Six months later, we turned professional together with his brother Tim, and moved into a bedsit at 11 Stanhope Road in Highgate, North London. I was 16-years-old.

The experience was brief. Soon afterwards, Roger was signed by the now legendary figure Joe Meek who had already established himself as a sound engineer over a number of years with unique recording techniques. Meek had graduated to being a freelance and independent record producer, first with his own 'Triumph' label and then with a space-age approach to pop from a tiny studio above a leather shop in north London. Roger was made an offer he could not refuse, and Tim and I were left to explore fresh fields.

Less than a year later, as part of *'The Tornados'* instrumental group, Roger was top of the charts in every country in the world. Sadly for him, it did not extend to riches. Distribution complexities and bad management accounting turned the enterprise into a shambles, and what should have been a financial bonanza for all concerned, stumbled and fell.

It certainly did not end my relationship with Roger, though. During the years that followed, he would appear from time to time either to borrow money or with the odd cabaret booking when he needed a singer and I fitted the bill. These varied from private party-type balls – often in country piles with large regal audiences – to celebrations of sorts onboard cruise liners while they were in port. They were always highly paid, and so I never felt the need or justification to ask him to return the loans that mounted up over time. On most of these occasions, there were big bands and even medium-sized orchestras booked for dancing, and one bandleader who had once been an international star gave us useful advice. Roger's role on these occasions was as a star guest, and while no one could tinkle the piano keys quite like him, he was limited with what else he could offer, and needed an addition such as me when it came to cabaret. These engagements paid extremely well, and the duration of his appearance was usually forty minutes. He had recruited me to do twenty of the forty minutes, and it was following one of these that the bandleader came up with his advice. He advised Roger to put together orchestrations for my contribution to the proceedings, so orchestras like his and others too could back me with greater effect. He went on to make the point that it would not only enhance his cabaret contribution, he could offer me out as a solo performer and take an agency cum management fee from me.

The outcome was not as successful as it could have been. Roger was never cut out to be an agent or in management. I did work with him on many occasions over the years and earned excellent money, but over time they became less and less frequent. Towards the end of our cabaret relationship, he would seek me out and find me in all sorts of obscure places; once, he even located me in a Salvation Army Hostel for vagrants.

*

Suddenly, I returned to the present, and reality.

I lay in a dreamlike state, my muddled brain attempting to work out where it had all gone wrong. When I was seventeen, I became a trainee merchandising salesman for a national company and, in two years, learned more about life than I would have in ten had I stayed in the confines of village life. Sadly, it was here where I learned how to drink alcohol, or rather *how not to,* depending on how you looked at it.

In the years that followed, I was dismissed by several companies as a result of alcohol-related misdemeanours, where my speciality was writing off company cars. I was always able to earn a musical crust or two along the way, and there were sober intervals where I worked at a high enough level to rub shoulders with established stars. Just the same, it was the amber nectar that proved to be my downfall, and by the early 1970's I was an unemployable nomadic alcoholic. Along the way, I married and fathered a daughter, but thankfully for them both, my wife locked me out of the family home with the help of social services. Following a straightforward divorce (made so due to the fact I was living in an old sandstone mine), she married someone who I understand made her happy for the rest of her life.

In my hospital bed, and looking up at the shadows that drew distorted shapes across the ceiling, my mind returned to the last time I saw her. I had left the sandstone mine which provided me with a lair of sorts and where I was still sleeping rough. As I approached the main road, I stood in a filthy state, waiting for the traffic to clear so I could cross. My blurred vision picked her out coming in the opposite direction, holding my daughter's hand on one side and the lead attached to my beloved mixed-breed mongrel on the other.

I tried to turn away, but my little girl's eyes saw beyond the filth and mess and greeted me as a daughter would, but something had shifted.

'Hello Daddy,' she smiled a beaming smile and skipped a few childlike dance steps, 'I can't stop; my other daddy is waiting.'

My ex smiled. It was almost apologetic but not quite, and she spoke a few words explaining the urgency for returning to her new home and husband. It was then I realised my favourite pet, who I had aptly named Brandy, was whining pitifully and straining against his lead in an attempt to reach me. She had to drag him hard until they were out of sight, and I watched all the way, crying tears that still return half a century later whenever I recall the memory.

3: TIME TO LEAVE

I got stronger every day; a fact made more noticeable due to the shocking physical state I had found myself reduced to. Over the course of three weeks, I'd had plenty of time to think, and I asked both doctors and nurses many questions about addiction. Candidly, I was shocked by the lack of knowledge required to offer answers.

My detox medication regime came to an end, and after a few days, the reality hit me that I didn't really know *who I was*. I was unsure of the real me. This was not memory loss; it was the way I thought and behaved, and my perception of everything around me and how I related to others. This version of me was kind, caring, responsible and completely bewildered by the person I had become as a result of the constant presence of alcohol. Then, in a moment of nightmarish recollection, I switched to how I had been changed when I drank alcohol. How my selfish ethanol-addled brain distorted truth, and the fantasy world it forced me to live in. I collapsed in tears and felt no shame; there was no need to as I did so in front of others who were treading the same road.

I revealed all in the exercise book CB had given me, and then to a lady psychiatrist. Later in the day, she loaned me a copy of '*Dr Jekyll and Mr Hyde*' by Robert Louis Stephenson with the words… 'Now read how much worse it can get!' It did not take me long to work out the author must have had hallucinatory alcohol experiences like mine to be able to put pen to paper and record this journey to hell! A pity he hadn't had the courage to spell out the obvious connection more specifically, I thought to myself.

Had he done so, it would have provided a stark warning to readers worldwide since 1886. Perhaps I could do a more modern-day offering, I thought to myself. If it's not too late, I added quickly before remembering George Eliot (nee Mary Ann Evans) who spoke the words, '*It is never too late.*'

I started to scribble some notes in my room during what was visiting time for the other nineteen patients. I felt conspicuous sat alone in the common room when all the others received their families. The circumstances of my confinement were the same as the rest of them, so I believed there to be a difference between me, my symptoms, and theirs. I just did not understand what they were, and I wanted to avoid facing up to them. A knock on my bedroom door brought an end to my exile.

'My name is Paula and this is my husband Tom,' she smiled a friendly smile as she made the introduction. 'My brother is in the next room and you have been kind to him, and so we thought we would say hello and thank you.'

I looked back over my shoulder at my current domain and decided it was inappropriate to invite them in.

'I'll come out and sit with you if you like,' I said, realising any other suggestion would have been absurd.

They were a delightful family and had a daughter the same age as my own little girl. There were moments of alcohol-withdrawal-type-sobriety amongst many roofless homeless drunks, when most would lament the losses of their children and often their wives. I was never one of these people; I spent the painful physical and mental hours thanking God my wife had found someone who loved her, and was happy to take care of them both. Subsequently, I forged a friendship with Paula and Tom that enabled me to feel part of a family. It has endured for a lifetime, and I am so pleased I met them.

*

A week later, I was discharged from hospital and reverted into my old and familiar drinking pattern almost at once. Deep down, I knew alcohol was at the root of all my problems, yet incomprehensibly I perceived it as the only friend and comforter I had left. In my alcoholic insanity, I reasoned that if this were to desert me too, I would be left with nothing at all!

It may have been for sentimental reasons, and I'm not exactly sure why to this day, but I had a sudden urge to return to my roots. I was a Black Country lad, and it may have been where I thought I might find peace, perhaps even compassion. The 1970s were friendlier days for the hitchhiker, and the first lorry I thumbed stopped, picked me up, and delivered me all the way to the heart of it.

Due to my homeless status, the hospital had given me the equivalent of half a week's wages at lower income rates, from some charity fund or another. I still had some left and headed for a pub I knew well. I approached the bar, ordered a stiff drink, and then scanned the small number of customers to see if I recognised any of them. I spotted Bob.

Robert Goodall was the smartest man I had ever met. He was very much in the traditional style, probably influenced by military service during which he had served as an officer. We always seemed to use the same selection of pubs with our respective partners, and both of us worked in sales. He was married to a delightful lady, and at first, I had a succession of girlfriends and then my first wife. I somehow took it for granted that I would bump into him twice a week or so, although we never actually knew each well. It was normal, therefore, to greet each other in the style of 'Hail fellow, well met'.

During the years when my drinking spiralled out of control, I lost track of Bob. I was barred from my usual pub haunts where I had built up debts to finance my habit, and deep down I knew I had become an embarrassment and a general nuisance. I faded completely from my usual scene and lost contact with all my usual drinking friends. Then, here today, even scruffier than I was, sat a sullen and unkempt Bob Goodall.

'Bob!' I exclaimed, surprised. 'How are you doing?'

'Piss off,' he replied rudely.

I was so taken aback I told him I certainly would not, and if he wanted rid of me, he would have to throw me out himself physically. I knew I was safe enough; he had just enough strength left to pick up his beer.

He shrugged and gazed firmly into his glass, seemingly in deep thought.

'So, now it's got both of us,' I said with a certain irony.

He gave me an odd look and asked what I meant.

'You mean you haven't realised your problems in life are all about drinking alcohol?' I announced, sounding full of wisdom I was far from convinced about, but which I'd learnt from my recent stay in the hospital detox unit.

The incredulous look he gave me could only have been genuine. He listened in total amazement as I told him all I had heard and learned from others about alcohol addiction. When I had finished, he spoke for the first time in half an hour. It was to tell me he had never seen his visits to the pub and considerable alcohol consumption as in any way an addiction or a destructive force which had cost him dear. It had never occurred to him any of his many problems were due to drinking alcohol. No one had ever suggested he drank too much, and it had never dawned on him that any of the company cars he had smashed up were due to alcohol abuse. The broken relationships, debts – even the death of his wife from liver failure – could all be connected to the staggering amounts of alcohol they had consumed together, but none of these things had ever crossed his mind. He had been sacked from several firms, and it had been said to him with conviction, '*Well, you <u>know</u> why Bob*,' but of course he didn't know why – not at all. Only now was he beginning to realise those with alcohol problems were often the last to know.

If I had told him he had won a major prize, he could not have been more delighted. He was as pleased as punch, and it was quite bizarre how he began making plans for a sober future in front of me there and then. It wasn't what I wanted to hear, and all of a sudden I couldn't wait to get away from him, so I made my excuses and set out to pastures less likely to abstain. I walked around for an hour or so, and as daylight faded into twilight, I felt a compulsion to go somewhere far away and start again where no one knew me.

A signpost pointed towards Birmingham and the M1, and it seemed as good an idea as any. After half an hour or so, an unladen medium-sized truck picked me up, and a friendly voice welcomed me to his world. He described his life as a fishmonger, which explained the smell which surrounded me, although if I'm honest I was used to far worse and did not find it objectionable.

'I do the Billingsgate fish market run regularly. My mates think I'm crazy getting up to drive down in what they say is the middle of the night,' he laughed loudly and I joined him. 'But do you know, I love it. There is a unique camaraderie between us, and I get to choose from the pick of the catch.'

The truck trundled along at a steady speed, his voice never seeming to stop; I was glad because I knew the longer he did so, the less time there would be for describing my sad lot. However, my turn arrived inevitably.

'I take it life isn't as good as you would like it to be?' The way he phrased the question made it easier to give an account of myself and my predicament. My appearance gave it away I decided, and it was possible I might smell worse than his fish truck. But if I did, he didn't comment, and it was only a couple of days since my last bath prior to hospital discharge.

'I'm a drunk!'

I'd never said the words out loud before, they sounded strange even startled me, and I didn't follow them up. I half expected the truck to stop and his friendly voice to change to one of hate and detestation, ordering me to alight in case I contaminated his forthcoming load of fish. Instead, his response was a jolt for any self-pity I might have had.

'Me too; haven't touched a drop for six years. I lost my wife and kids and nearly my sanity, then I found Alcoholics Anonymous and although I didn't take to it as an ongoing thing, I saw and heard enough in a couple of weeks to scare the shit out of me! Have you tried it?'

'It's not for me,' I replied, but added instantly, 'One thing I do like about it, though, is when I'm in a room with fellow suffers. I feel like I'm with my own sort… does that make any sense?' I looked across at him and could see his head nodding in the semi-darkness, accompanied by a sigh.

'I'm very aware of the ignorance and lack of understanding from doctors,' my new friend lamented. 'And how – when you do get offered treatment – it's always AA which, of course, is free. I have a doctor pal who I met at an AA meeting, and *he* talked of the stigma affecting him from a professional standpoint. He also had many theories of serious medical conditions he believed alcohol was the cause of. He said we needed to research the possibilities much better.'

My truck driver's closing words on the issue will stay in my memory forever. He said, 'Think about it… what if alcohol was at the root of many cancers, and the main treatment for it was in the hands of the local plumber, labourer, sales rep, shopkeeper, and whatever other occupations are represented at AA meetings?! It would be a bloody farcical situation, wouldn't it?'

We chatted on a different basis now; it had become an even playing field, and for my part, I could be myself. As for him, I suspect he saw much of his former self in me.

We arrived at Billingsgate Fish Market and he took me into a 5am opening pub, opposite, called 'The Cock Inn'. He gave me a ten-pound note, put the price of a couple of pints behind the bar to complement the first one he'd bought me, and then departed to conduct his business.

'Good luck, mate,' he said as he departed. 'Don't let it kill you!'

4: DARK DAYS

I considered my predicament from every angle following my meeting with the fish man.

I walked for miles around the crowded streets of London, looking at various shop windows and sniffing hungrily at the different food aromas that wafted from countless eating houses. No matter what the time of day, Earl's Court, where I finally found myself, was always milling with people, and soon I was tired of being jostled and walked into a pub to buy myself a fix!

'Yes, sir?' The barman's voice caught me by surprise and I ordered a pint of bitter, the chat with my fisherman friend at the forefront of my mind. It lay on the counter for several minutes. I tested myself to see how long I could go without, and eventually noted it had been at least two hours. Then it was in my hand, and I was drinking the liquid greedily. An hour later, I was drunk and awoke in the early hours of the next morning at the bottom of some filthy concrete steps. I climbed them painfully and found myself on a demolition site of sorts. I was surrounded by rubble and other debris and craved a drink to rid me of the ghastly withdrawal and deaden the pain of… I knew not what! I rummaged through my pockets and was elated to find a five-pound note and a stack of change. I thanked God but wondered if it should have been the Devil.

All I craved was another drink to rid myself, even if only temporarily, of the chronic withdrawal which I saw as retribution for failing to heed the warnings once more. I staggered towards a busy street I could see in the distance, despite blurred vision, and headed for the nearest tube station and booked through to the Monument.

Before 6am that day, I was throwing back a brandy in the '*Cock Inn*' opposite Billingsgate Fish Market. Three days later, I had lost my overcoat, spent my money and stood, filthy dirty, with four other down-and-outs by a wood fire at Spitalfields Vegetable Market. The story was the fire had originated after the end of the first Boer War when many former military men returned from battle and were homeless due to wounds both mental and physical.

Sympathetic market workers let the victims keep warm by supplying non-returnable wooden crates and cases as firewood, and the practice continued and the fire burned until the late 1970s. It proved to be a haven for me on very bleak occasions, until the shock of a vagrant woman giving birth in clouds of wood smoke shocked some reason back into my head.

With the help of one of the others and then members of the public, we got her to hospital, but I have no idea of the outcome. I did try to visit her, but for reasons that only registered in later years, I was not allowed in!

Hours ran into days, weeks, and months all filled with drunken insanity, in a world where I clung onto people – just like me – who had given up on any hope of normal life and living. Somewhere along the line, there was a Christmas. On occasions, I noticed drunken humans from a world where I once lived. They were well-dressed but staggered drunkenly, smart clothes askew, on their way home to face the berating of an angry wife, four hours late for dinner! I wondered how many of them would eventually join the ranks of sub-humans like me, who would then think the same of another generation coming up behind them. It was a well-trodden journey to Satan's den.

I had stayed in the best hotels and used classy bars, then mediocre boarding houses and shabby pubs. Flea-ridden flophouses followed with cold, deserted and outdated bars. Ultimately, there were doorways or cold, windy and often rain-soaked public parks, and finally, archways under viaducts on skid row, drinking meths and hooch, made from industrial substances and liquids.

In my alcohol sodden spectral delusions, when I was homeless in London Town, I had nothing, but all night long my imaginings convinced me the deserted streets were mine.

5: MEETINGS WITH DESTINY

I made many attempts to kick the dreaded booze, frequently inspired by my own writings in CB's exercise book, which was nearly full. I was constantly on the move, occasionally doing odd jobs when I was capable, and this enabled me to buy second-hand clothes, although it was far more likely I would *borrow* a sleeping vagrant's coat. I became convinced only someone who had been inside the head of an alcoholic vagrant could unlock the formula of a successful awareness and recovery programme. I needed a way out of my hell. I decided I wanted to be *that* person and began to spend hundreds of hours researching in libraries, and begging interviews with doctors and others from the medical fraternity. I recorded every word and shoplifted another exercise book when CB's was full.

To their credit, most people agreed to give me the time of day, and a pathologist – himself a recovered alcoholic – risked a great deal by allowing me to sit in on autopsies so I could see alcohol damage from the inside. All the time, I collected information like a sponge absorbs water, accumulating the life stories of dozens of homeless drunks I met either on the streets or in the overcrowded hostels of the 1970s. I now had several exercise books full, and kept them in two carrier bags. Yet, through it all, I remained an active alcoholic, revolving between hostel beds, shop doorways, and much worse!

One early Sunday evening, three days before Christmas, and feeling extremely ill and confused, I stood in the darkness of a suburban city street gazing through a window at a family of four sitting around a table having tea.

Mum and Dad were dressed casually but traditionally, and two little girls who could have been twins wore identical dresses and laughed a lot with parents joining in, although no sound came my way from *their* secure place.

I was enchanted by the scene, and a sudden voice which was firm but not threatening did not distract my fascination.

'Is there anything I can do for you, sir?' it said.

My eyes remained riveted on the domestic scene, my concentration transfixed; nevertheless, I replied to the voice.

'You could tell me why I can have none of this,' I asked, pointing at the happy family scene.

I felt a hand on my shoulder; it was warm, not rough and made me shiver slightly. I wore only a shirt and trousers, and the sensation of heat reminded me I was cold.

The hand became an arm around my shoulders, guiding me across the roadway, which formed part of a square. There was a bench; we sat down together, and the voice which was in uniform spoke again.

'I'm Sergeant Campbell. Tell me about yourself.'

I could still see the family, although now they were further away, and a white concrete pillar partly blocked my view. I told Sergeant Campbell of me… non-stop.

I came to an end, and silence reigned; the light had gone out in the family home, they had adjourned to another safe place. I'd had my say. It was my new friend's turn now, and he spoke in a tone that was rich in wisdom.

'You have told me in detail many of the tragedies you have endured,' he said softly. 'The bad luck, the dirty tricks and failed schemes, you say you can't even have a drink without getting drunk. You are baffled by what has become of you. You were the one with all of the talent and promise, and now you have nothing and no one! But I wonder, perhaps, if it's *not* that alcohol is *one* of the problems in your life, but that *your* problem in life *is* alcohol!'

Suddenly, the message behind the good cop's words penetrated my distorted senses and, indeed, my very soul. Less than half an hour previously, I had felt grateful for being able to have a drink. I had been robbed of everything, but at least my dearest friend – who lived in a bottle – was always there for me during the bad times. Now, I was facing a terrifying possibility. Was it conceivable that alcohol could be a tyrannical despot that had deluded me, perhaps a nation, and maybe even a world, into believing in an illusion? That all on its own, alcohol was the greatest delusion maker of all! Had it, in fact, been conning me for years and indeed mankind throughout history, magnificently convincing the human race of ideals that were fatally flawed?

I remembered a study that sarcastically aligned the 15% of the adult population who were teetotal as being a sad group, the people who were missing out on all the fun in life. Then I deduced this would mean 85% of the adult population used a legal drug regularly. Simultaneously, I recalled my childhood and wonderfully reliable family members who got sillier as drinking evenings wore on. Sometimes, the fun would end in arguments, even rows. Normal people turned into something else… by alcohol… their friend…?

The good Sergeant had been looking through the information in my carrier bags using the light from his torch and then suddenly made a decision.

'Most of the hostels have closed their doors for Christmas,' he said, 'but I believe in you, and I may be able to secure you a place in one where I know the man in charge. But only if you would like me to?' I nodded and thanked him.

Sergeant Campbell walked at least two miles out of his way and, as promised, used his influence to secure me a bed.

*

I didn't know it was 1975, yet that first night in the hostel system was unforgettable. Fifty men slept in a former workhouse dormitory, beds two feet apart. The smell was putrid, an unforgettable pre-death stench of dying flesh and stale booze. On one side of me was a WWI veteran; on the other, a former officer decorated on D-Day. They spoke in slurred tones of their respective battles for a better world. Ironically, they were Tom and Harry, so together we were Tom, Nick, and Harry. I managed a smile to myself.

As I lay there, with so many other lost souls in those long-gone days when such emergency accommodation was commonplace, an extraordinary sensation swept over me.

To the background of life's casualties and their night-time ravings, I discovered the definition of vocation. I realised each and every one of us lying there in the darkness needed an answer to the same question, but there was no point in asking because we knew no one had the solution, at least not the one we wanted to hear. There and then, I decided the time had come to collate the information from my alcohol studies at the grassroots level in hostels, marry it all up with life and experiences I had witnessed living rough on the streets, and compile a work for the good of mankind. I would be the drunk who would unlock the mystery of the inner world – the favourite living place of the alcoholic.

A distant clock struck twelve, and I boarded a midnight train to salvation. It would be a journey that would take more people with me than I could have imagined in my wildest dreams.

6: GOOD CAME FROM THE SS

Having discovered how the city hostel system worked, in the New Year I found myself in and out of it depending on my sobriety. Being either too drunk or too dirty was reason to be refused admission.

On this particular day, I had been excluded and stood in a queue at the homeless handout office in Stepney, known to all down-and-outs as the "SS", mainly because they had to make ruthless handout decisions. It was a cute concept inspired by it being Social Services, and was situated in **S**carborough **S**treet. Christmas, meanwhile, had come and gone.

Amongst the chatter, I heard word of a Dr Weiser in the East End who ran a practice of sorts for the homeless, and I decided to make him my next stop in the hope that he might understand my mental state. I found him easily enough. I consulted a couple of dossers swigging from a bottle of cider on some waste ground, and they knew who I meant immediately. One of them put a grimy hand on my shoulder and turned me around with surprising strength to face the opposite direction. He pointed at what had once been a terraced row of shops, now deserted and one step away from demolition, and to one place in particular. It had the word CAFÉ in faded letters above a battered frontage, and yards of tape crisscrossing the inside of the glass frontage, synonymous with wartime.

I told Dr Weiser my name was Nick; it was all he asked of me, and I got to know him well. He played an important role in the lives of many London vagrants, and I suppose – for a short time – I may have done so too. His surgery, if I dare call it that, was as broken down as his clients were, and would never have survived in the modern day. Yet, the foundations to the next four decades of my life were about to be laid in this grimy place. I knew at once he could penetrate the mysterious wavelength and mentality of the alcoholic vagrant. It was a priceless comprehension he would never have been able to describe to his comfortable colleagues, who sat in their ivory towers at the Royal College of General Practitioners.

'What is it that you have in your carrier bags?' His words were delivered with a slight Eastern European accent, and he didn't hurry me for a reply. It was as though he knew they were the inner sanctum containing the soul of a homeless dosser, plus a few other mysterious possessions. In reality, I was thinking how his accent sounded full of wisdom.

His eyes stared over ancient wire spectacles that reminded me of Pathe News film showing holocaust images. In them, similar glasses were piled high in such places as Auschwitz, Buchenwald, Belsen, and other extermination camps, alongside other once-treasured possessions. I wasn't ashamed and answered him at once.

'They are full of exercise books and notes on bits of paper; I have been researching alcohol addiction through the lives of people like me for about four years.'

'Why?' He spoke the single word with a twinkle in his eyes, and I knew at once his reason for asking was not critical or threatening.

'The medical profession knows nothing about alcohol and the power it wields over the masses.' I paused momentarily to check out his reaction, but the twinkle remained in his eyes and so I continued.

'Alcohol has been around for thousands of years and has baffled medical science, in its various forms, for all of that time, and they are no further forward now in how to deal with it than they were at the very beginning.' Now I was on a roll and on the edge of my chair, my withdrawal forgotten.

'Do you know, there is evidence that two hundred years ago in the Mediterranean mountain villages, all the kids were lined up when they were around eight years old and given a vessel containing their traditional wine? The village Elders would then pass along the line to see the reactions from each child, and it is said they could spot immediately those for whom the alcohol performed the devil's magic! In other words, they knew perfectly well it carried more threat for some than others! And all from individual reactions!'

The good doctor kept his eyes on me, and I continued. 'I remember vividly how I reacted more manically to a pint of beer than my mates in the early days. If only those Elders had tapped me on the shoulder when I started drinking. It is this lack of understanding and fundamental learning that took me from polite and meaningful society and dumped me – and too many others – onto the streets as unemployable wrecks!'

Suddenly, I felt faint and acutely nauseous. I told Dr Weiser so, and he reacted at once. He stood up, quickly defying his age, opened a wall cabinet and took out a small bottle of pills, then filled a glass with water from a tap directly below it and handed me two.

'I want you to take these now and drink all of the water slowly,' he announced before adding in a controlled tone, 'I will treat you starting right now if you will do something for me…'

I looked at him, puzzled.

'I have nothing to offer you, I'm afraid,' I said miserably. 'I haven't even got the strength to clean up the mess in your office,' I added, looking around me.

'You could be a lot worse than you are,' he replied. 'Most of my patients are too far gone to notice it, and those that do attend wouldn't be here if it was smart, clean and modern! This tells me you have a way to go yet. But, unless you hear me out, you will surely achieve your aim of self-destruction.'

'I'm listening, doc.' I tried not to sound like an actor playing a part and his response suggested we were both having the same thoughts.

'The time is not now for you to think you are striking a business deal of any consequence. It will suffice for you to believe that you are simply in the right place at the right time.'

It reminded me of how I felt, long ago, when my headmaster at senior school took me into his office and informed me I would never get into the school soccer team because I was not good enough at outplay… but I was the best goalkeeper they'd ever had in my age group. If I chose to play in goal, I would be the first name on the sheet every week. I never did play again for the first team because I stubbornly refused to play in goal, and had regretted my stupidity ever since. I would never show the same stubbornness again.

'Would you allow me to borrow your notes just for tonight? Maybe, I will be able to learn from them?' Dr Weiser looked serious, but I knew he could not possibly be. I paused, undecided how to respond.

In the first two years of their history, I had studied and made notes from every addiction textbook I could lay my hands on, and copied so-called expert's words of wisdom out in longhand. I then systematically tore their written words apart. I set about reworking addiction as I truly believed it to be, from my suffering and that of others who confided their deepest secrets in a way they would never do to a doctor.

With my notes and the confidence I had taken from a bottle, I eventually approached a teaching hospital reception, clutching a bag of selected observations and asked to speak to the doctor in charge of alcohol addiction. A smart lady receptionist asked me the nature of my visit, and I told her the main man had much to learn from me, and I had brought along the evidence. She informed me he had studied at the very best places of learning, and she could not possibly bother him with every Tom, Dick and Harry off the street that arrived without an appointment. I must have been offended and retaliated loudly because security guards arrived and, in those days, they were not gentle in their requests for you to leave. When I sobered up, I realised I must have sounded ridiculous and looked even worse, standing there in clothes I hadn't taken off for weeks. It was ludicrous for a sober me to imagine my carrier bags contained anything earth-shatteringly valuable to the medical profession, and I sank into deep despair for many days in the knowledge that my research was in vain. That night, I stuffed two years of study into a waste bin in Trafalgar Square and walked back to my usual place of refuge under a viaduct on the Thames embankment. A few days later, a fellow dosser – known to street people as Simple Stanley – gave them back to me. He said he recognised the carriers and knew I would never part with them; would there be a reward? I gave him my tobacco tin, filled with dog-ends taken from the streets, and he was delighted! Bless him.

On another occasion, and in a mood of despair, I deliberately left them on a tube train… and they got back to the hostel before I did! I'd forgotten my name and hostel address was written in several places, and a kind lady member of the public had gone out of her way to return them.

'Well, are you going to answer me?'

Abruptly my eyes re-focused on the old doctor, and I nodded. 'I think there is something you should know though, Dr Weiser,' I managed.

'And that is…?' He seemed to be drawing on reserves of patience.

'The truth is,' I struggled, 'I think writing it all gave me a sense of purpose, maybe even importance. Some of those I interviewed thought I was researching for the NHS and believed it might help them in the long run, too, and I played along. The lady at Bishopsgate Library didn't think I was a waste of time, though; she always went the extra mile for me and dug up all sorts of facts and figures. I couldn't have done a lot of it without her. I need you to know that some days I think I am deluded, and they are a waste of time, but somehow I just keep writing as though God himself is forcing my hand.'

'Do you believe in God?' The words were quick-fire, and they hung in the air waiting for my reply. He waited and clearly had a great deal of patience, and I knew I had to answer. When I did so, my voice was firm and steady.

'Yes, I do, but I don't think he loves me. At least not right now.'

'Have you considered he may have a plan for you?'

Now I got angry.

'What sort of bloody plan would mean I had to lose my wife and daughter, and parents too?'

He pointed at my carrier bags. 'You may be carrying around God's work. Perhaps your studies will help thousands like you in the future? We all have a job to do here on earth, you know… more or less!' The doctor looked deadly serious.

'But there are tens of thousands of words, and some people I have confided in think they are the ravings of a lunatic!' I protested. I knew I sounded desperate but then I was, and yet deep down, I knew I had not written them for my benefit but in the hope my hellish experiences would ultimately be for the good of all.

'Why don't you let me be the judge of them?' Dr Weiser looked like he believed in me, and so I told him he could.

'If you think it's all rubbish, will you be kind enough to just give them back to me and say nothing?' I must have sounded pitiful, but he nodded and said, 'I promise.'

His last act of the day for me was to telephone the hostel and tell the top man I was on a detox and request I be allowed to return. This was granted and I did so armed with four more tablets together with instructions on how to take them. I'd had to promise to return and see him the following day at 1pm. He probably knew it was a safe bet; after all, I had entrusted with him my worldly goods.

*

I cannot begin to imagine what modern-day health and hygiene inspectors would have made of the many hostels I frequented. However, to people like me, they were an absolute godsend. Street people typically take a while to degenerate to sleeping rough in dreadful and unimaginable conditions. You rarely go from central heating and well-equipped bathrooms to a 6´ x 2´ rectangle under a viaduct, or scrunched up double in a shop doorway. It is a slow journey where conditions deteriorate without you realising it. After either of these options, the hostels of the day were palaces, and not as cold or dangerous as doorways or park benches.

They were, after all, refuges for life's casualties. They were better than a cold and painful death, alone and discarded by humanity, although only just. The hostel that Dr Weiser got me back into was a building that housed two hundred and fifty men and boasted six toilets, two baths with taps hanging off, and one shower, which was only capable of dripping slowly.

At dinnertime, served in a vast area down two flights of stairs in what had once been a cellar (and which smelt like busy urinals), I met Sam and Dave, two street buskers who admitted to being hooked on heroin and weed. They asked me warily if I had any good drug connections. I shook my head, said I was sorry, and explained my poison was booze.

'Yeah, booze kills me too, and I think I've done summat to my stomach. I went through a patch when I drank Polish stuff made from industrial polish by murdering bastards who too often kill off their customers with the first sale.'

It was Sam who had spoken. He was studying me as if trying to decide if I was trustworthy, or perhaps able to contribute to their next cause, whatever that happened to be. I nodded down at their guitar cases which were propped up by an empty chair.

'I suppose you ain't got a spare one of those?' They both looked at me with fresh interest.

'Do you play?' This time it was Dave.

I needed to tread carefully; this could go either way. Frequently a turf war existed at places where lucrative cash could be picked up, and I wasn't looking for trouble. The problem was I'd been a professional singer in another life and I was good, at least I had been, and now – even on a bad day – I could run rings around their kind.

'Yeah, I do, but I'm probably not up to your standard. I could help out though if it earns me a few quid,' I offered with false modesty.

Sam reached forward, picked up one of the cases and handed it to me.

'Play us a riff or two and then sing summat country.' They both sat back in their chairs and stared at me expectantly.

The instrument was crap and way out of tune, but I had a middle C etched deep into my brain and soon got it shipshape. Then I pulled back from the standard set by the last big band I'd fronted, did a fancy intro, and gave a verse of country rock. Even at this well-below par performance, they failed to hide their excitement.

'We can definitely pull some dough! You sing and we'll go round with our hats. Is a three-way split okay? Sam was good to go, and Dave was nodding furiously. I said I was happy with the arrangement and asked about the venue.

'You make it sound like a bloody cabaret booking,' Sam was grinning broadly. If there had been a hint of hostility in the early exchanges, there was no sign of it now; it was as though we had been friends for a lifetime.

'Tube stations work, Tower Hill too. There are tourists there even this time of year, and the Americans are loaded and generous,' Dave sounded confident and got to his feet. 'C'mon, let's make a move,' he added.

'I've got a hospital appointment at 1pm tomorrow, so I can only do till 12.30pm. Shall we call it a trial run?' They were disappointed but accepted it had to be that way.

We headed up the first of the two flights of stairs, and as we turned a corner to negotiate the second flight, we had to walk in single file in order to pass by a bundle of rags that suddenly moved. I flinched instinctively and Sam chuckled. 'It's only Johnny Two Gobs. He's harmless.' I looked back and for the first time saw a head which appeared to be resting solitarily on top of the pile of rags which I know realised were his clothes. The head had eyes that bore a haunted expression made worse by a large piece of bloodied and discoloured sticking plaster covering one cheek.

I was now playing catch-up as Sam and Dave had moved a few paces ahead of me while I had been studying the cause of our encounter.

'Kind of sad,' said Dave, 'He's got some sort of cancer from drinking crap. It's eaten a hole in his cheek and he's refused treatment although it has been offered. When he eats, he has to hold the food in from the outside with the palm of his hand until he swallows it. He's not allowed to eat with the rest of us cos of the mess it makes, so he sits there until we've all finished and then they allow him in and give him squares of newspaper to clear up afterwards.'

*

The busking went well the following morning, and by the time I left, my share was well worth the effort. I had to run all the way to Dr Weiser's surgery to make the 1pm appointment, however. The street busking partnership lasted for a month, and then we fell out over something or other, and Sam and Dave moved on.

Johnny Two Gobs died by his own hand some months later. The story was he left a note saying he hated his life of hell and humiliation, and he asked God to forgive him as a postscript. It was pinned up on a notice board near the exit door where everyone could see it, and I said a prayer for his soul and asked that he be forgiven for whatever he had done to deserve his lot. I often wondered, afterwards, that if my suffering was so I could help others as Dr Weiser intimated. What on earth must Johnny Two Gobs have done to deserve his wretchedness?

I decided to write up his story and add it to the works in my carrier bags. Then, if some good came out of it all, at least he wouldn't have suffered and died for nothing.

7: WEISER'S WISE WORDS

I arrived at Dr Weiser's surgery breathless but at precisely 1pm, and as I entered noisily, he stood with arms held out before him in welcome.

'I am so pleased you came back, Nick,' he said with feeling. 'In my world, few do unless they have to.' I didn't reply because I didn't know what to say; after all, I *had* to return if I wanted my carrier bags back.

'What did you think?' I asked, nodding towards where they stood on his desk.

'Considering you are a *homeless, alcoholic vagrant*, and I quote from your own words,' he said pointing at my carriers, 'You are the first person I have ever met who speaks on the same level of understanding concerning alcohol addiction, as I do.'

I experienced a warm sensation like I had when I was told I had been made a Prefect at school; only his voice brought me back to the present.

'I have never seen observation, deduction and approach to match it,' he continued, 'although much of it is in rough, and I am sure you won't need me to tell you so, and there is a great deal of discussion required to decide how to use it. Only someone who has endured – in the way you have – could have written in this way.'

Dr Weiser took his seat. 'Do you remember me suggesting you could do something for me if I treated your alcohol withdrawal?' I nodded nervously as he pointed to an area of his surgery room immediately behind me.

'See that door in the corner?' I turned around and noticed it for the first time.

'Yes,' I responded.

'Go and have a look and then come back.'

The handle was stiff, and the door scraped the frame, making it difficult to open, but the surprise came with what it revealed.

Opening the door revealed a large storage space – probably from when the building had been a café – but closer scrutiny suggested it may even have been a large eating area, of the sort that wasn't quite a restaurant. In the middle was an ancient cast iron wood or coke furnace with fuel access from the top. It had a circular round chimney leading out from the back and then abruptly upwards to the roof. Twenty or so chairs encircled it, which stretched to two tiers, and the roof itself looked like it had been patched up many times. Unexpectedly, Dr Weiser's voice interrupted my thoughts.

'There is an open invitation for all the homeless people to come here and socialise each Saturday night. I offer cakes and sandwiches, and the only stipulation is no alcohol or drugs. Two of my former patients who are serving police officers come in plain clothes to make sure law and order is kept, although I've *never* had any trouble. In a strange way, I think the majority of the homeless are appreciative of my efforts, and they enjoy getting together in the warm. If I'm honest, it gives me a buzz to be able to add human warmth to their existence.'

'Did the coppers have a drink problem? I mean, is that how you met them?' I sounded puzzled because I was.

Dr Weiser smiled and beckoned me back to his surgery, leaving me to struggle with closing the door behind us. Only after we had resumed our previous positions did he speak.

'Do you remember writing the section in your works where you criticised the general public's attitude towards the drunk? You said there will never be equality amongst alcohol users until we eradicate the word alcoholism from the English language. As you wrote, it draws a line in the sand and no-one will admit, even to themselves, that they have crossed it due to the stigma that lies beyond.'

'Yes,' I replied. 'The word alcoholic is a big part of the problem. People's alcohol consumption is all about degrees of addiction. It's not black or white.'

Dr Weiser smiled as I got into my stride. 'Users drink for effect. If we extracted the ethanol from alcoholic drinks – and offered it pure – few people would like the taste enough to purchase it, manufacturing would cease. The brewers and distillers would be out of business overnight. People drink because… alcohol is a drug!'

Dr Weiser nodded in agreement, and there was a pause.

'You still haven't told me what you want me to do for you,' I said to him, with the biggest smile I could muster.

'Ahhh, yes! I wondered if you would do a talk for me at my little get-together on Saturday night. Something on your experiences and your desire to record it all for the good of others? I could arrange a few questions and I can tip you off about what they are beforehand if it would be of any help.' My smile must have slipped because he added, 'It's not the London Palladium, you know; you never quite got that far, did you?' I shook my head… he really had read all my notes.

'I'll do it,' I answered. 'I'll even help with the sandwiches if you'll let me.' There was no way could I refuse such a small favour requested by this lovely man… the dosser's only friend! I already owed him substantially more than he had requested!

'Done,' he said joyfully. 'Now, I'm free for an hour or so; how say we go and have a belated lunch at the café down the road and we can chat about your carrier bag notes?'

'Done,' I said, purposely copying his style.

*

Dr Weiser secured his surgery well enough but said everyone knew he didn't keep anything valuable there, least of all medication, and it was all safe.

We walked a few hundred yards, made a few turns here and there, and then entered a smart eating house that seemed somewhat out of place for the area we were in. He was made very welcome and so was I.

It seemed he had a regular table, and as we sat down he told me I was the first patient he had taken there. It gave me an unfamiliar feeling of pride, and I wondered why me but decided not to dwell on it.

'Now, I would like you to tell me about Absinthe,' he began. 'I scanned it last night, but I'm intrigued. I'd like to hear it from you in your own words.'

For the first time in a long time, I felt bright and alive.

'In its original formula form, it was linked to flights of artistic genius and madness. Even now, it remains banned in most countries and has been for decades, but those who crave alcohol are looking for the ultimate hit, the easiest way to get drunk! Its reputation does the rest!'[1]

I took a sip of water and then continued. 'I spoke with a scientist who explained how Thujone seriously interferes with neurotransmitters; it creates a mysterious clarity of mind in those inebriated by it. There is a theory that Robert Louis Stephenson received a bottle of Absinthe as a birthday present, drank it all and passed out. The story goes that he had a hallucinatory nightmare and, as a result, put pen to paper on his now immortal tome, 'Dr Jekyll and Mr Hyde!'[2]

I paused for a moment to provide a little dramatic effect. 'It may be of interest for you to know, I am perhaps one of the few living souls to have tasted the original Absinthe formula and returned, although not completely unscathed, to tell the tale.'

Dr Weiser gasped and looked at me in amazement. 'How on earth could this have come about?' he asked wide-eyed.

'It was a year or so ago. I was in an alcohol withdrawal haze and had not eaten properly for some time. I was walking along a waterfront somewhere on the east coast where lots of boats were moored, when I noticed a board announcing one of the owners had a weekend's work for a 'Coastal Dive' operation. A ruddy-faced seaman type in a captain's hat was coiling rope on the deck, and I hailed him as loudly as the last dregs of my drunken reduced strength would allow.'

'Do you still need an extra hand?' I asked. He eyed me up and down without stopping his task with the rope, then finally asked, 'Can you cook?'

'Like Mrs Beaton,' I responded.

'Who's she?' The seaman looked serious.

'You need me badly,' I said decidedly, and then with a new confidence, 'Show me your galley list?'

'You'll do,' he answered back, clearly impressed by the fact I knew what a galley was, or maybe even a galley list, 'Come aboard, and I'll show you around.'

'Anyway, he gave me a conducted tour without blinding me with sea science, which was just as well, and then said all I had to do was stick to basics, no vegetarians and nothing fancy – breakfast, lunch, dinner and supper if required for a sum total of ten crew which would include me. The galley was well stocked, so I told him to count me in.

It turned out the boat was going to be diving on a 19th-century wreck three miles offshore. The rest of the crew arrived slowly in ones and twos and, whilst an odd bunch, were harmless enough; they certainly made me welcome. I did a cheese, onion and vegetable omelette with fries for tea, or dinner as they preferred to call it.

Having finished their plates, they showered me with compliments as I cleared the table. I returned after finishing the washing up where I declined their offer of brandy and much more, before the captain called for order.

'Do you know what Absinthe is?' His question was greeted by silence and the shaking of heads, which included mine. After an appropriate pause, he continued. 'I've had a tip-off from a friend. At the Harbour Inn, I got to hear about a hitherto undiscovered wreck with bottles littering the seabed, and some still visible in the hold.' He shifted his sitting position, lit a cigarette and continued. 'The description of some of the bottles match early Absinthe…'

In the restaurant, I took another sip of water, revelling in my story-telling.

'On the boat, the company laughed and some even clapped hands. Then a lady with large teeth interrupted, 'And if we find more than one sealed bottle, do we get to sample it?' she asked. The captain didn't reply.'

Dr Weiser seemed absorbed. 'So, you found Absinthe on the sea bed?' he queried.

'A dozen bottles. All corked and capped with lead tops. The first one to be opened revealed a black evil-smelling sludge, the second less so, and the third was perfect. The captain allowed us to share it equally between us.'

'And?!?' asked the good doctor eagerly.

'It was an unforgettable experience. A *rocket fuel hit* with all the symptoms of being extremely drunk almost instantly, yet with total clarity of mind. I vaguely recall the opening of a second bottle, and then a third, and I floated high, met up with Miss World, married her, and settled down in the stockbroker belt of a town where we had three beautiful children, and I drove a Ferrari… all in a few hours or thereabouts.'

'Then what?'

'I returned to reality in a rat-infested slum building many miles inland with little recollection of my maritime experience, and *none* of how my relationship with the rest of the crew ended! And I have suffered with migraines ever since!!

*

'Is it the usual Doc?' The waiter came over to take our orders. For a brief moment, I thought his words sounded disrespectful but the Doc's reply cast it from my mind.

'Yes please, Pedro,' He turned to me and pointed to a menu card on the table. 'I'm a vegetarian and usually have the same dish, but please choose what you wish,' he stated generously. I picked up the menu to cover for the fact I had been struck dumb and needed to buy time. Nobody had bought me lunch, in a proper restaurant, for a very long time. 'I'll have the same as you if I may Dr Weiser.' With a hand half-masking his mouth, he whispered, 'Call me Doc, most people do,' I nodded and only then did I notice I was holding the menu card upside down.

Dr Weiser smiled broadly and spoke with a sincerity I was still not sure I deserved. 'How do you intend to put all your research – all those pages of work – into a recovery programme, Nick?'

It would have been impossible to describe the confusion in my head at that moment created by life on the streets, an insane place coexisting within the real world. It would not be a simple task to put into words the mega disturbance my rational thinking had endured, and so I took the easy way out.

'I'm way off right now,' I replied. 'There's so much material as you know, and I need to collate it into some sort of order. Hostel life is not conducive with such luxuries.' He studied me hard, stroking his chin, as if he was trying to make a decision. When he replied, I knew he had seen in my work a potentially valuable product.

'You may use the spare desk in my surgery, but only by arrangement. In an emergency, you would have to leave at short notice; is that acceptable?'

I hoped he hadn't seen the tears of emotion in my eyes, and I was relieved the waiter re-emerged at exactly the right moment. Somebody cared!

'Thank you, Doc,' I managed with difficulty, 'I hope my ability to do the job is up to the faith you have shown in me.'

'One condition. I really don't need to say out loud, but I will anyway,' the Doc's voice was soft but stern, 'one drink and you're gone.'

I didn't need to reply.

---

[1] History and the purists will tell us that the modern-day version of Absinthe cannot be compared with the 19th and early 20th century product. It is said, in some quarters, that the original chemical formula of Thujone (which is an essential component in the product) has been lost over time. Its modern-day counterpart has been reduced in strength, and as a result, the dangers associated with the Absinthe of old have lessened. Others believe that legislation has prohibited excessive amounts of Thujone. It has been claimed that Absinthe contained 260-350 mg/L of Thujone previously (1895–1910), an amount now deemed excessive and hugely dangerous. In the modern age, it has been limited to just 10mg/L! This would certainly explain why as an alcoholic drink it once had such a ferocious reputation and was involved with confusing and contradictory laws; for example, in some countries it is illegal to sell it but not to import it. If the inclusion of Thujone was not enough, Absinthe also contained pure wormwood oil which, when tested on animals causes seizures, independently from the effects of the potent

alcohol. The two together were always going to be a lethal combination.

[2] Absinthe has perhaps inspired both hallucination and myth. It certainly seems to have been the *in drink* towards the end of the 19th century when it was the beverage of choice for artists and poets like Oscar Wilde, Toulouse-Lautrec, Edgar Allen Poe and Pablo Picasso. To a man and perhaps even woman, they were all searching for extensions via fantasy to enhance their existing talents.

8: DEFINITELY NOT THE PALLADIUM

All things considered, I was remarkably calm when I awoke in my hostel dormitory on Friday morning. I decided to forgo breakfast and take an early stroll and Dr Weiser had said he would be at his surgery around 9am. It was agreed I would arrive soon after to take him up on his kind offer of the second desk to put my Saturday talk together. As I entered the beginning of the condemned Spitalfields area, I spotted a leaflet pinned to a lamppost advertising my Saturday address. Before I had taken twenty steps, I counted half a dozen more, roughly secured to doors that would never open again and on windows where there was still glass. I smiled nervously to myself at the Doc's faith in me, and swore an oath under my breath not to let him down.

'Some geezer who's supposed to be one of us is doing the talk,' the voice from behind me said, and I turned to see who the owner was. 'It just says Nick on the leaflet,' he added. I looked him up and down, he seemed friendly enough, and I decided he was around the same age as me, except tubby and wearing glasses held together with sticking plaster. 'Are you going to go?' he asked.

'I ain't got a lot of choice,' I replied simply, 'cos if I don't go, there won't be a talk… I'm Nick!'

'So, you fancy yourself as a bit of a star, do you?' He wasn't being unfriendly, his grin was as wide as the Whitechapel Road, and he looked like he needed a friend not confrontation.

'Are you going to come?' I sounded like I wanted to make sure I had at least an audience of one… and maybe I did.

'Not a bloody chance! I'll be on the piss somewhere having a goodun!'

He sounded like a kid looking forward to Christmas.

'Well… that will bring with it the promise of suffering,' I commented, and he looked at me over his broken specs.

'What the fuck's that supposed to mean?' He still didn't sound aggressive, just curious, and I thought I might have touched a nerve.

'How long do you think you're going to survive for if you go on living like this?' I asked, qualifying my statement while looking at him squarely.

'Don't tell me you care whether I live or die?' he shot back, squinting behind the specs.

'As a matter of fact, I do,' I said and turned away. 'See you tomorrow night,' were my final words, which I shouted loudly over my shoulder, 'and don't be late!'

*

Dr Weiser was already behind his desk, and I had to stand to one side to allow four others like me to leave the premises before I entered. 'Morning Doc,' I offered, and he gestured to a small table where there was an electric kettle and some decent mugs that seemed out of place in the surroundings.

'Good morning, Nick. I've cleared the desk I promised you and put the carrier bags by the side of your chair; let's start with some coffee, shall we?'

I can only describe the way I felt as surreal. I had been homeless for four years, and it had been a long time since I'd heard anything referred to as mine. I never gave a thought to my tramp or vagrant-like appearance, and it had been ages since I had given it any thought at all. Following the Doc's words and the emotional impact they had, I looked at my reflection in a sizable mirror he had hung on a free section of office wall space. I saw a complete mess – a person I hardly recognised – and wondered how many of his other visitors got a shock like mine. Then I realised it was there for a purpose; one glance was where the treatment started. My next consideration was that if I looked like this from the outside, then what was the inside of me looking like both mentally and physically? I certainly felt ill a lot of the time, and frequently suffered acute pain in many areas of my body; but the answer had always been a drop of the hard stuff, and then I no longer cared.

'Good morning, Doc. How are you today?' I ventured, hoping I hadn't taken too long to answer him.

'I'm fine, thank you Nick,' he responded. 'Don't forget the coffee.'

The electric kettle roared away and having discovered he liked two spoons of sugar, as did I, we were soon chatting on our favourite subject… alcohol.

It was amazing how much difference a proper seating position and flat surface made to my writing quality and quantity too. Not only did I complete my Saturday presentation for my homeless counterparts, I even began a series of others I thought may provide the framework for my treatment programme.

I must admit the earlier thoughts in relation to my physical and mental decline had sharply brought into focus another worrying consideration, and I decided to address it while I had the opportunity.

'I would like your opinion on an issue, Doc,' I ventured. 'Many people like me have had wives, families, and even regular employment, yet slowly – due to our love for alcohol – it all slipped away. Someone once asked me *how* I could have found myself sleeping out in the cold, rain, even snow, and my reply was, you don't go from central heating to a cardboard box or worse. It's a slow decline, and you accustom yourself to it by degrees. It's not that you don't feel the cold, of course, you just accept it as a way of life, but it is a slow process. What I would like to know, Doc, is do you think there is a point of no return? A stage where we couldn't readjust to a normal life again even if we wanted to?'

The Doc's hands wrestled together, and his face screwed up in different expressions as he strived for an answer. He stood up, then paced the floor back and forth like a man tormented by indecision, and I was beginning to worry I had asked a stupid question to which there was no answer. Then he responded in a serious tone, revealing his hesitation was to protect me.

'In your many notes, you wrote a section where you described the point of no return; do you not remember this?' I shook a bewildered head and he continued, possibly to divert my attention and save me from the misery of recognising yet another significant episode of memory loss. 'You described it as the favourite living place of the alcoholic and went on to say there are, in fact, two points of no return. The first is when the drink claims you for its own and you cannot live without it; and the second is when it takes you beyond redemption, from where you cannot claw your way back no matter how much you want to.' He looked me straight in the eyes. 'I'm worried,' he continued, 'you may be closer to it than you think, Nick.'

*

I had arranged to meet the Doc at his surgery at six o'clock on the Saturday evening, and I arrived promptly. I had expected to be a bag of nerves, but instead, I was calm to the extreme. It was as if I had been preparing the script over many months, and knew I was absolutely word perfect.

I was greeted warmly in more ways than one. The Doc had obviously fired up the furnace much earlier, and the large room was unimaginably comfortable from the way I had first seen it. Also, he had company. Two delightful ladies from the civilised world, clearly dressed down for the occasion in sloppy sweaters and baggy trousers. I wondered if they might be their gardening clothes and smiled to myself, then felt ashamed; the fact they were there at all made them special, maybe even dedicated.

'Meet Molly and Delia; they're drunks just like you. But they escaped the streets by a hair's breadth. This is Nick, who I have been telling you about, ladies.' Wrong again, I thought to myself.

Both women approached me together, with faces lit up by happy smiles. No handshakes here; instead, huge and undeniably genuine hugs and Molly even put the flat of her hand at the back of my head and briefly held it hard to hers.

'We've heard so much about you, Nick.' It was Delia who said the words while Molly nodded furiously in agreement, still retaining her smile.

'Follow me and I'll show you what we prepare each Saturday,' said Molly, practically dragging me towards two trestle tables pushed together end-to-end against one of the walls.

By any standards, it was a feast, and momentarily I was overcome by the Doc's generosity and overwhelming dedication to his street people patients. My emotions extended to these two delightful women and provided me with all the proof I needed that there was life after destitution.

'I had a few nights out in the winter chill, Nick,' Delia offered, I thought, by way of identification. 'I'm three years alcohol-free now thanks to the Doc who got me into a hostel,' she added brightly.

'Two years for me,' chimed in Molly. 'I was a bit slower at breaking away from it than Delia, then I lost my digs and was lucky enough to meet Doc the same day, and he got me into a hostel too. I have secretarial skills, and after he was convinced I was serious about staying sober, he got me a job in a hospital, and I'm still there.'

'Have you any plans right now, Nick?'

'Funnily enough,' I answered, almost quoting Winston Churchill, 'I think this might be the beginning of the end… of where I am at present.'

'Is there anybody there?' A male voice came from the direction of the Doc's surgery, interrupting him from carefully placing the chairs in a circle around the furnace.

'Coming,' he replied, before hurrying in the direction of the voice, 'It's only Alfred,' he explained momentarily, 'he acts as sort of doorman on Saturday nights. Finish the chairs off, please, Nick. Just follow my pattern.'

*

In no time at all, there were thirty men and four women gathered – not counting the Doc, Molly, Delia and me – and most of them were familiar faces.

When everyone was seated, the Doc stood and introduced me as Nick, one of their own street people, and told them he had invited me to do a talk.

I got to my feet and was about to begin when a late arrival appeared – the man I had met the day before with glasses held together with sticking plaster. I raised my hand. 'It's okay, Doc, he's a friend of mine and he's late for everything… except when the pubs and off-licences open.' For a moment, I was startled when laughter erupted and even scattered handclapping, then my entertainment skills kicked in big time. This was not a high I would ever find in a bottle!

'How many of you know Bridget the Midget?' I began. There was an immediate reaction and I had to call for order. 'One at a time, please, gentlemen!' I shouted and pointed at a tough character I knew by sight. 'You first, Sir.' Laughter broke out again and a voice shouted loudly, 'He's been called a lot of things, but Sir ain't one of them.' The mirth increased then slowly subsided, and the man spoke in an educated voice.

'I know her and I think you'll find most of us do. She loves being called Bridget the Midget, and she's not very happy if you don't, although she'll settle for Bridgmidge if she's in a good mood.'

I thanked him and addressed the room. 'I guessed most of you would know her, but I wonder if anyone knows why you haven't seen quite so much of her during the day recently.'

'I heard the council got her a flat,' said one voice. 'Somebody told me she'd got a fella,' said another. I thought that was enough and continued my talk.

'Well, we're about to find out. Bridgmidge gave me an interview – a case study – for my research that most of you will have seen me carrying around,' I paused to allow for some muffled laughter, then held my notes firmly due to a slight trembling of my hands, and read with a confidence which seemed to have survived despite the ordeal of recent years.

'Bridget was three foot six inches small and an alcoholic homeless vagrant,' I began. 'She sat daily, on the wall of an old cemetery at the beginning of Whitechapel Road at Aldgate East in the heart of London's East End. Her little legs would dangle over into the street, and she would watch the early morning rush hour traffic as it battled to get into city offices each day.

'Most days, she reserved her only change of expression for a distinguished-looking man in his mid-fifties, who sat elegantly in the back of a chauffeur-driven Rolls Royce. It began with a slight pucker of the cheeks, developing as the days went by, into a full grin and eventually to a cheeky wink and a hearty wave. The gent seemed to look forward to the encounters as much as Bridget. Without doubt, she would not have missed them for the world.

'One terribly cold winter's morning, the pattern changed. The man pressed a button, the electric window whirred silently, and an outstretched hand offered a pack of cigarettes to the tiny figure sat on the wall. She paused for a moment – this small area of the East End stood still – her eyes shifted from pack to man and man to pack and back to man again.

'I don't smoke them, mate,' she lied in broad cockney.

'The man's arm sagged slightly in the middle but remained outstretched.

'Perhaps you know someone else who would like them?' he offered.

'Yeah! Okay then,' she said but remained seated on the wall.

'Neither of them spoke for a moment, his arm began to sag in the middle, and then she broke the silence.

'How tall are you?'

'The man seemed surprised. 'Six feet exactly,' he said.

'Well! Would you jump off a twelve-foot wall?' She smiled and a grin spread over his features as he got out of the Rolls, reached up, and pushed the cigarettes into her hand.'

The sound of my audience's laughter was sufficient for me to wait for the appreciation to die down before I resumed with even greater confidence.

'The daily ritual continued, hardly changing for several months, then one morning, for Bridget, life should have changed forever. The gentleman alighted from his Rolls Royce, the usual pleasantries were exchanged, and the pack of cigarettes was offered with an outstretched hand, but today was different.

'I've bought you a present,' he said kindly. 'She looked at him closely in anticipation of the prize, and then gazed around him at the back seat of the car in an effort to see what was on offer; she saw nothing. He beckoned towards the empty seat.

'I'm not getting in that bloody car with you,' she uttered rudely.

'How can you come to harm with my chauffeur present?' he asked logically.

'You gotta be joking, mate!' Bridget grabbed the usual cigarettes and scampered off. Her benefactor got back into his car, somewhat irritated, and waved the driver on.

'The same scene was repeated the following day, and the day after that, but on the third, Bridget was waiting with four very undesirable looking companions.' Laughter broke out again amongst the group, but this time a voice piped up loudly.

'I know that's true mate, I was one of the four and most of this lot didn't believe me, did you?' He looked around and some even looked sheepish; I thought it time to resume.

'I'll come mate,' said Bridget, 'but me oppos here have got your car number.' The man smiled as she got in and the car about-turned and headed east towards Stratford.

'Bridget looked spellbound; her mouth wide open. The flat had two bedrooms and was purpose-built for someone of her stature. She could reach every conceivable part of the complex thanks to raised floors and specially designed cupboard space. The door handles were two feet from the tastefully carpeted floor.

'During the weeks that followed, Bridget could be found most days busying herself in her new home. She would sometimes be accompanied by a street friend, whom she could often be heard to bully into keeping her home neat and tidy.

'At seven o'clock each night, however – come rain, hail, snow or storm – she would look proudly around the flat, brush off the last specks of dust, carefully lock the door and return to sleep in the park at Aldgate with her street friends.

'So deeply ingrained had her alcoholic, vagrant existence become, it was *impossible* for her to think of life evolving in any other way. She had passed the point of no return.

'The mysterious man had meant well. Bridget still has the keys to her flat, proof of her ownership lies in a sideboard drawer, but he no longer passes Aldgate Cemetery.

'He can sometimes be seen doing a detour a couple of roads to the south of Whitechapel Road, and he never looks up from his morning paper.'

*

I'm not sure what sort of reaction I expected, but it never occurred to me it would be none at all. The Doc didn't react, and because it was not like him to behave in such a way, I thought he would have a reason. So I sat down and scanned everyone's faces. A minute can be a long time, and this was a good example. Then the well-educated voice sounded out again.

'I suppose most of us thought we couldn't sink lower than the streets; it couldn't get any worse, so to speak. But Bridgmidge… well… she's proof positive there is further down than street level. You've convinced me, Nick. Absobloodylutely!'

'Me too,' said someone else. 'And me,' said another and similar words echoed around the room.

The Doc had an expression on his face I hadn't seen in him before; it was a mixture of achievement, perhaps satisfaction, or maybe a little of both tinged with elation. He broke out of his stillness – 'Supper is served' – then came over and whispered in my ear excitedly. 'I think together we have taken a major step forward this evening, Nick.' The remainder of the proceedings was taken up eating the excellent buffet put together by Molly and Delia, and I spent time talking to both of them jointly and severally.

Molly was the daughter of an alcoholic mother and had been married to a sales executive. She'd had two children, and her husband had divorced her and won custody of them in a messy court case. She had subsequently drunk her way into homelessness and a women's hostel.

Delia had been a teacher in an upmarket boarding school for girls and could render no explanation as to how she had succumbed to alcoholism. 'I just did,' was all she could offer. 'I concede I became unemployable if that's any help,' she added.

*

The hostel dormitory brought me down to earth with a bump when I returned to it at the evening's end and realised I was in a difficult situation. I desperately needed a place of my own in which to settle down, but I required proper employment in order to secure it, which would continue to elude me without a kosher address. I decided it would be a long road back to normality; after all, I had invested many years degenerating into my current state!

My last thought prior to finding sleep was that permanent sobriety would undoubtedly provide the key to normal life and living – absobloodylutely!

9: A GIRL CALLED GINGER

Working at the Doc's surgery – on my treasured carrier bags full of alcohol facts, figures and case histories – had somehow overcome an all-too-often craving to drown my sorrows in copious amounts of alcohol. However, on the Doc's advice, I restricted my working week to three and a half days as he felt I was an all-or-nothing person, and as a consequence, my passion could diminish and, at worst, I would burn out. I had far too much admiration for him to contradict his assessment despite my disappointment, and on reflection, decided I may have seen evidence of this happening myself. I remembered the two occasions I had discarded my bags as a waste of time, or as a fantasy trip during which I was set on saving the world. Each time they had been discarded, they were mysteriously returned, and I had thanked God. I did so again, now, but with the conviction it really was leading somewhere and meant to be.

Living in an overcrowded hostel and not drinking alcohol meant the nights dragged on inexorably, and I often walked the streets. On one such night, I came across a food and hot drinks caravan parked in a side street near Spitalfields Market. This street was a mecca for the night people: workers on night shifts, lorry drivers, and the inevitable dossers, loners and losers. Ordering a mug of coffee, I perched on a nearby concrete post and watched the others milling around. It crossed my mind how the average man or woman would never rub shoulders with the lower end of this company, and I smiled ruefully because I fitted neatly into the wastrel section. It wasn't even that long ago when I had been employed by multinational companies, and was capable of entertaining at any level.

'Hi, do you mind company?' The voice was soft, cultured and did not seem to match the appearance of the young woman who had approached from my blind side.

'I can manage a coffee if you like, but that's about it,' I answered.

'I haven't seen you around here before,' she continued, seemingly oblivious to my words. I decided she had once been quite pretty, five feet six, thirty-something, a mop of carroty-coloured hair, and a figure going to seed. She seemed to blend in well with the rest of us at the lower end, but I was suspicious of her intentions; living my life had made me wary of almost everyone.

'It's my first time here,' I responded honestly. 'The coffee's okay, and I may come again.' I turned to leave but was surprised by what came next.

'Please don't go.' The voice had a note of desperation. Suddenly, she seemed embarrassed. 'I'm sorry,' she whispered and turned away. I watched for a few seconds and then surprised myself with what I did next.

'Hey, Ginger. Wait!' I broke into a trot and was soon stood by her side. 'Look, I'm sorry if I seemed offhand, even rude, but…' I continued.

'That's okay,' she interrupted, and then I realised she was fighting back tears. 'I just felt like some real company and you looked more decent than…' her voice trailed off as she looked around her, and tears overtook the words.

'Please don't cry,' I managed. 'Do you live around here?'

She nodded. 'Would you allow me to walk you home… if that's in order?' I offered, quaintly sounding like the local vicar. She must have thought it old fashioned too, even Edwardian, and we laughed together in simultaneous realisation as our thoughts clicked. She recovered first and spoke graciously… 'That would be nice.'

I offered an arm, and she slid hers through it as if we had known each other all our lives. We talked as we walked, and with her in close proximity it became clear my perception that her figure had gone to seed was created by clothes, which had once been her size, now hanging from a skeletal body due to weight loss.

We took a shortcut across some wasteland which was strewn with demolition debris, and Ginger pointed it out, speaking breathlessly.

'When I first came here, all this was shops and houses, and over there is the old Spitalfields School.' We stopped to look at the weird spectacle of street lights still functioning on roads going nowhere, and then she added, 'There was no-one living here, of course, but there are legends that still hold good, of local people refusing to leave because their families had lived here for generations. By all accounts, some stayed put until the bitter end. The famous East End wartime spirit no doubt,' she added and then concluded, 'One of the workmen told me the street lights remain connected to enable them to work later and make the area safer.'

Soon, civilisation beckoned and we crossed a main road holding hands. Then she let me go and turned up a side entry.

'This is my palace,' she said with a smile nodding at a heavy wooden door. 'Would you like to come in… err… I mean just as a friend?' I hesitated, but she didn't seem to notice and opened a battered handbag and drew out a key. The door opened easily, and she entered and then looked back at me with a quizzical expression. 'You don't have to come in if you don't want to.'

It had been a long time since I'd had a female friend of any sort, and an hour previously, we hadn't even met. I think I lacked confidence and even wondered if I was shy. Suddenly, I made a decision. 'Yes, I will,' I even sounded self-assured.

It was a small bedsit but practical and adequately heated by small radiators. The main area acted as a dining room and lounge. It had a neat facility which appeared to be a cupboard, but pulled down to reveal a double bed providing a triple purpose in one space. But it didn't end there. Ginger tugged on a chrome handle set into a wall and a worktop slid out silently, uncovering a metal framework that supported a platform upon which sat an electric kettle and a Baby Belling cooker. A further door led to a small shower room and toilet. As a contrast to the modern appearance of everything else in the property, two comfortable-looking club chairs stood in close proximity to one another. I chose one and sat down while Ginger busied herself.

She explained there were four small units like hers which had been renovated from an old office building, and which were owned by a housing association. 'I consider myself very fortunate,' she said, looking and sounding proud.

'Right,' she announced, 'tea or coffee? I recommend coffee 'cos the milk is tinned.' I laughed and nodded; she filled the kettle and it was soon roaring away.

'Tell me about you,' said Ginger brightly, as she joined me on the adjacent chair, having handed me my coffee in a mug which matched her own.

'I'm a bank manager,' I said, and we both laughed. She looked quite pretty when she laughed, and I told her so.

'All the boys chased after me in another life,' she remarked. Abruptly her laughter evaporated and her eyes were sad again.

'How old do you think I am?' she mumbled, almost inaudibly.

I never knew quite how to handle questions like this, and yet for some reason, diplomacy seemed unnecessary with Ginger. 'Between thirty and thirty-five,' I answered truthfully.

'I'm twenty-four today.' Her head was bowed forward and she spoke the words into her lap.

I accepted the information, showing no surprise, and neither did I offer an apology for being ten years on the wrong side of reality. Then I gave her an abbreviated version of my life and times, as she had requested, including my fall from grace at the hands of the bottle.

'How did you get to find this little hideaway?' It sounded as if I was deliberately changing the subject, and I suppose I was. She seemed to ponder, unsure on whether to re-enter a life lost, and so I offered a little encouragement.

'Perhaps it would be helpful if you talked about it,' I said. Long ago, I had attended a counselling course – in error – for a couple of hours. I was looking for an AA Meeting in a council office building and turned right instead of left. I hadn't got the confidence to walk out when I realised my mistake, so in those two hours, I learned to *let your patient talk*, and when they stopped, wait for a while to make sure they really had. Today, I was trying it out.

A small wisp of red hair had curled forward onto her forehead and she studied me for at least half a minute before responding.

'Would it sound corny if I told you that it all began a long time ago?' She whispered the words, holding my gaze steadily while simultaneously holding her mug of coffee close to her lips.

'My father owns a large haulage company business north of the Yorkshire Dales, and I was brought up in beautiful countryside. It was a lovely house with flower beds and well-kept lawns. We had a lovely swimming pool, tennis courts, and Daddy had exciting landscaping plans... I was to attend the Sorbonne, but something terrible happened!' As she was talking, I was preparing to laugh loudly at her equivalent of my bank manager joke, until she uttered the final words. They stopped me dead in my tracks.

I had heard *many* stories in the course of filling my carrier bags, and I had never been in any doubt about those which were basically true and others that were fantasy or wishful thinking. On this occasion, I knew I was about to hear this young woman divulge her personal, true life, nightmare tragedy.

'I was young and innocent.' Her voice was barely audible, and her pale skin, synonymous with red hair, was blushed with embarrassment.

'I was invited to a Christmas party in Paris by a French friend who lived there; we were best friends and had met at boarding school. Mum and Dad were against me going but I got my way, and to be honest, I was uncomfortable from the moment I arrived. I don't want to go into too much detail right now, but the place was awash with alcohol, and there was a great deal of drug-taking. Fired by alcohol and the drugs, things got rough and during the fracas I was held down and forcibly injected with heroin. The next thing I recall was being surrounded by gendarmes, and then nothing until waking up in hospital feeling like hell with Mum and Dad sat each side of my bed. I was kept in for 48 hours and then flown home in a privately chartered aircraft, accompanied by my less than impressed parents.

'The French police wanted to take proceedings against four young men, but my father's hotshot lawyer advised us not to press charges. He said it would be a dreadful ordeal for me with such limited recollection, little evidence, and only a limited chance of me identifying them. For sure, I didn't want to relive any of it, and in reality, I would have been a lousy witness. When our lawyer said – all things considered – he could not see how the French could possibly get a conviction, the whole thing seemed a horrible waste of time, and that was the end of the case… but it was not the end of it for me.'

I looked up sharply, unsure what was coming next, but before I could speak, Ginger carried on.

'A few weeks later, I discovered I was pregnant. I couldn't stand the thought of facing my parents, and so I packed a case while they were out, drew out my savings, and headed for the railway station without any clear plans. I took the London train mainly because it was the next one to depart, and if I'm honest, as it pulled out of the station, I was overcome with relief. They were such wonderful parents, and in my temporary insane and probably shocked mental state, I believed they would be better off without me and I could save them from my shame.'

Ginger paused and I felt I had to say something. They were the days prior to legal abortions, and I thought I would add words of practicality.

'It was a different time and they were different days,' I offered sensitively. 'Days of shame and pride, based on the rules and teachings of the time.' She reached out and gripped my hand.

'On arrival, I booked into a hotel and that night walked to Soho, which I had read was the red light district. It was a calculated risk, but I thought one of the working girls might be prepared to point me in the direction of a back-street abortionist. Nothing is straightforward, of course, and it took a week, but in the end I got what I was looking for. Naturally enough, the girls were wary of me at first and probably suspected I might be a plainclothes policewoman, but I made a friend out of one of them eventually and she gave me an address. She described it as 'Grottsville' and it was no exaggeration! Worlds away from what I was used to; honestly, it was truly horrible! A scruffy flat, no proper hygiene; an old woman bent almost double probably from osteoarthritis let me in, and I was scared to death. I've never felt so alone in my life.'

I tried to make sympathetic noises and even pulled appropriate faces, but I knew nothing matched the utter hopelessness and helplessness I felt for her in the moment. I told her to stop if it was too distressing, but she shook her head and soldiered on, ignoring my plea.

'The abortionist was an elderly man who took my money first, seemed completely devoid of any feelings whatsoever, and left immediately afterwards. I was left alone in the charge of the old biddy who told me to stay in bed and she would make some tea. I swallowed some painkillers, was grateful for the warm liquid, and cried myself to sleep.

'When I awoke, the flat was empty. I left hastily, hailed a cab and returned to my hotel, only stopping briefly to inform reception I was not to be disturbed and would call down if I needed anything. When I awoke, it was mid-morning the following day and my body ached literally everywhere.'

I let go of Ginger's hand, stood up and filled the kettle to make more coffee. Ginger stayed silent for a long time, gazing into space. I began wondering how many stories like Ginger's and mine there were within a couple of square miles of where we were… given the hostel and homeless population.

I decided not to attempt normal conversation and would wait to see if she had unloaded all she needed to say. I put her coffee by her side, and she sat up, said thank you, and began again.

'There is not much more to tell. I was on heroin for two years and made no attempt to contact home. Then, after an overdose and a hospital admission, I entered into a detox plan using methadone. So far, it seems to have worked. I've been heroin-free for eight months, but now I want to stop the detox medication too, and I am going to see someone tomorrow who I've been told is an expert when it comes to addicts. I think I might be ready to stop completely.' I was thinking back over her words when she suddenly laughed shrilly, and sat up straight in her chair.

'Do you know what? I haven't the faintest idea what your name is!'

Her upper-class or perhaps educated accent wasn't always in evidence, lifestyle can change that over time, but unexpectedly it had revealed itself clearly in every syllable.

'Nick… My name is Nick,' I found myself saying, somewhat surprised that I hadn't said so previously.

'As in Nicholas?' she enquired.

'Yes, absolutely, but I actually prefer Nick.'

'Are you a junkie?' Ginger looked at me questioningly, and even threateningly, with neither her upper-class accent nor educated tone in evidence.

'No, my problem is alcohol. One glass is too much, and a lorry load is nowhere near enough.' Ginger exhaled air noisily through pursed lips and was noticeably relieved.

'My God,' she said, with the Sorbonne beckoning once more, 'in God's name, how could I have omitted to ask this of you?'

I knew exactly what she meant. Had I been a drug addict like she was, I would have been a major threat to the task which faced her when coming off methadone (should a friendship develop). My reply was standard and well documented somewhere in my carrier bags, and I touched on it now in my reaction.

'I've done a great deal of research and writing on alcoholism, and in truth some of the realities spill over into drug addiction. In many ways, they are worlds apart; after all, a different state of mind is required when a criminal act is involved. But an addict, no matter what their poison, has a mountain to climb if they are to make a full recovery. If two addicts are attempting to recover together, you could argue they both have to climb the mountain twice.'

'You sound like an expert, Nick. Tell me more about your life,' she said after a lengthy pause.

'Okay, I will, but I have a suggestion.' Ginger looked at me quizzically.

'I do a bit of busking and have some money left; let's go round to the late shop and buy some bits and pieces. I'll cook you something to celebrate your birthday!'

Her face lit up immediately. 'That would be amazing; Are you really serious?'

'Of course I am,' and for a moment I actually felt embarrassed. 'C'mon, you idiot,' I blustered, and we set out together.

*

I was quite a dab hand when it came to cooking, and I managed to come up with a halfway decent curry under the limited conditions. It turned into a feast for both of us.

Later, at the meal's end, Ginger begged me to tell her my story. She had been to a few meetings for alcoholics to support a friend, and some of the experiences she had heard were dreadful.

I felt unusually relaxed as I nursed a fresh mug of coffee and began to describe my life. It was easy to confide my insanity when compiling the events onto wads of paper and in many exercise books. I thought it would be an ordeal to recount my life to a relative stranger out loud, so it came as a complete surprise to discover the words flowed in a way I could never have imagined possible.

After relating several violent incidents, I mentioned there were amusing situations too, and she urged me to tell her one, her eyes alight in expectancy.

'Well, there was one I was thinking of…' My memory raced back over the years and I chuckled loudly at the recollection, which only made Ginger more excited at the thought of hearing it. 'Pleeeeeease!!' she begged.

I pulled a teasing expression and made myself even more comfortable.

'It happened one year just before Christmas. As per usual, I was in a hostel for homeless men and on the twentieth of December I telephoned my father with a coin I had found on the pavement. I asked him if I could come home just for Christmas Day. He responded with a 'No!' and would not accept the charge when the money ran out.'

'How sad for you, Nick,' Ginger's voice seemed strained, but I was not to be put off, and this story had an amusing twist. The entertainer in me was on a roll.

'I was scruffy, but not dirty, and had spent many hours that week wandering around gaily decorated shops and stores to keep warm, bewildered by and large by my exclusion from the festivities. What was so different with me that I could not be part of this?

'As extraordinary as it sounds, I was *glad* I could drink alcohol. At least I had some comfort, and I thought it probably kept out the cold. I remember pondering on my lot, struggling to work out why I was different from other people. I would look at others going about their daily routines and wonder why I could not be like them. It wasn't as if I hadn't tried hard enough, and people seemed to like me at first. I could tell from the way they spoke to me when we had a good drink. Of course, I couldn't remember everything the next day, so I presumed I had offended them during the course of the evening with my behaviour. Mostly they avoided me from then on, rarely ever making contact again.'

'I know what that feels like.' This time, Ginger's voice was supportive and I began to enjoy telling her my tale.

'Jobs, always assuming I could get one, never lasted more than a few days and often only hours, and I realised it was occasionally because I fell asleep on the job. More frequently, management disapproved of the newfound confidence I achieved with the aid of a drink, and misinterpreted it as me being argumentative and offensive. I was slightly disturbed by the effect alcohol had on me, and my personality seemed to change more than most people's, but *everyone drank*, so I attached little importance to it. Then, over Christmas week, I got lucky. I was in a city department store by Santa's Grotto when the poor old man was suddenly taken ill, leaving a queue of waiting children. A smart man – obviously the manager – appeared panic-stricken, and without hesitation, I stepped forward and offered my services.

'I'm out of work,' I explained. 'You could soon make me up and stick a beard on, and if you like what I do, your problem is solved.' Ginger's laughter was so loud it almost drowned out my words, and I paused wearing a broad smile.

'Anyway, he considered it only for a moment, and then I was bustled into a staffroom, painted and rouged by a couple of female staff members, and dressed in Santa's familiar garb.

'The job itself was really quite splendid. I had a stack of toys at my feet and a glass of sherry on a silver tray – for the *mums* – which I poured from a stock beneath where I sat, at the top of the stairs with my back to the bannisters.'

This time Ginger shrieked in mirth as I soldiered on. 'Naturally, I joined each mother in a glass of sherry, and after a couple of hours I ran out. It may have been this somewhat irksome aggravation which made me lose my patience, but I think – with hindsight – it was more likely because the child on my knee decided to have a pee.'

I paused.

'I later explained to the police that I did not say, 'Take your shitty-arsed, pissy kid and chuck it in the friggin' river.

'I also maintained it was not my fault if the bannisters were of such bad workmanship that they collapsed when I leant against them and I, together with thousands of pounds worth of Christmas tree lights and display stock, fell twenty feet to the landing of the floor below.

'I also explained to the station sergeant I was a member of an espionage ring, and had been set up by the CIA.

'He definitely believed me because he told me to go away, or words to that effect, and celebrate Christmas on some other poor copper's patch. I wandered out into the cold night air and spent the rest of the festive season wondering, once more, why I had no family to share it with!'

'Oh my dear God,' Ginger was breathless with laughter and rubbing her aching sides, but I decided to end my factual recollection with what I considered to be an extremely sombre message at the time it occurred.

'When I was discharged, the arresting officer said something that gave me much food for thought. His words were quite prophetic, and they have lived with me ever since. He said, 'Never mind, son, Once in Royal David's City…. there was probably a drunk!'

Ginger's reactions while I had related my story had shown all the emotions. She had stifled laughter, suppressed tears, and shown expressions of irony; now, she left her chair and gave me a genuinely affectionate hug.

'You should write a book, Nick,' she said, and momentarily, I thought it was time I finished the carrier bags full of notes I had started so long ago.

We went on, late into the night, discussing each other's problems and addiction in particular. We agreed it felt good to talk to someone else who could identify with addiction at first-hand, above all, the aspects of physical and mental suffering.

Eventually, it was time for me to go back to the hostel. I had arranged a late pass, but there were still rules of conduct, and I didn't want to be too late as it was bound to have an effect on the night porter's schedule.

After making arrangements to meet two days later, I said a modest, or perhaps shy, goodnight and Ginger stood in the doorway as I walked away.

I gave her a cheery wave, and she remained there until I turned the corner out of sight.

10: MAMA, DADA, VERA AND NICK

I've hated mornings for as long as I can remember, although I'm unsure precisely how early in my life this came about. Given the amounts and obscure variations of alcohol I have consumed, I am amazed I can remember anything at all, and while doubtlessly there are swathes of experiences (and therefore memories) lost forever, some seem as recent as yesterday.

One such nightmarish recollection was the homeless hostel foreman walking rapidly through each dormitory at 7am, accompanied by the first few chimes of a distant church clock. The rest of it was obliterated by the sound of a football referee's whistle – which was his way of informing us he wanted the premises vacated. He always began at the top of the four-storey building and the closer you were to the ground offered varying degrees of warning. However, if you were near to the summit, the penetrating sound had the capability of making blood run cold! When one day I asked a rough, tough-looking character why the top floor got it first, his reply was just as threatening, 'If he started at the bottom, he would have to pass dozens of evil tempers on the way back down. Starting at the top means he's been and gone before anyone has the chance to lynch him!' Such was the way of things on the highway of lowlife.

I worked out – as near as I could – how long it was since my last drink, and decided it was my third or fourth week but with very little hope of complete accuracy. One good sign was when sobriety kicked in I became fully aware of the conditions surrounding me. The morning after meeting Ginger was a good example of this; the despicable odour in the hostel's sleeping quarters was overwhelming and made the prospect of breakfast unpalatable. I checked my meagre finances following the shopping expedition for her birthday dinner, and found there was enough for coffee at a cheap café, and possibly beans on toast. I had alighted from the last of the concrete stairs into what passed as reception, and was about to step into the fresh air when a voice hailed me.

'Wait, Nick, I've got a message for you.' George was almost always at the desk in reception sat behind thick glass, but now he had left it and was approaching me waving a tatty piece of paper. I took it, thanked him, and stepped out into the street taking a deep breath as I did so, while unravelling the crumpled-up message. It read… *Pop in ASAP-Weiser*

I changed direction immediately, and headed towards Aldgate roundabout and Commercial Street which led to the Doc's surgery.

'Good morning, Nick. I'm so pleased you got my message.' The Doc looked genuinely pleased to see me and even relieved.

'I've got an important detoxification to set up today and have all sorts of tiny but vital details to put into place. My problem is I've managed to double book, which in effect means I have dug a hole for myself. What I want to know is if you would do my counselling appointment with a man called Ken, leaving me free to make the detox arrangements.'

I was staggered and sat looking at him in disbelief, then decided I'd better say something. 'What on earth can I do for him? I don't have any of his background and I haven't a clue how to counsel anybody!' I knew I sounded desperate and I was.

'Well, you may not have realised it but you counselled thirty odd people last Saturday night, and both the ladies and one of the men have asked me if they could speak with you on a one-to-one basis.'

I was dumbstruck.

The Doc continued. 'I don't know whether you've realised it or not Nick, but the way your notes are written, they can easily be broken up to support counselling sessions. All you have to do is link them to a theme. I only made a quick calculation, but I reckon there may be as many as fifty…. all things considered.'

'How far have you got with Ken… in the recovery programme?' I asked cagily, wondering if my question might be regarded as an imposition.

He stroked his chin, as I had discovered he always did when he was not sure what to say. When he did reply, I was shocked. 'Truth is I don't have a programme,' he admitted. 'At least not one tailored to fit alcohol addiction. You see, when we were training – in my day – there was nothing other than the odd mention of liver damage which was alcohol-related. Sad to say little has changed in the modern day. You can't get an A-level and certainly not a degree in alcohol addiction treatment.' Dr Weiser stared in my direction and the only sound was the traffic passing by.

'So how do you treat them?' I realised I was looking at him with an expression of incredulity, and quickly tried to change it to surprise without success.

'I'm saddened you should discover it in this way, Nick, but why do you think I am in such awe at my discovery of your work. You may as well know I'm tempted to go out on a limb and say, in terms of potential, you may be sitting on something groundbreaking. Given a little luck and the wind blowing in the right direction, it could even change the way the medical profession views the alcoholic. One thing is certain Nick, the medical profession – especially GPs – are in urgent need of information like you've assembled.' Stillness reigned supreme, and then to himself (and I suspect unaware I could hear) he added, 'But I mustn't let them know it was created and compiled by an itinerant vagrant patient.'

'The upshot is, Nick, just do your stuff. Just like you did when talking to me, and like you did last Saturday.' All of a sudden, he was back to his usual buoyant self and I nodded along, feeling good as well as nervous.

'I won't be far away if you need me,' he added. 'I will be seeing Karen, my detox patient, at 1.15pm, here in my surgery should you need me for any reason. But I know you will be fine. I just know it.'

Dr Weiser straightened his tie subconsciously.

'One other thing. I've put you in the big room but I lit the fire early and by the time Ken comes at 1pm it will be as warm as toast. Right young man, I'm going to treat you to breakfast.'

*

I was pleased to accept Dr Weiser's offer of breakfast at a nearby café, hunger pangs were now in evidence and I ate heartily. Then, without warning, he asked, 'What can you tell me about Nalorex?' I looked at him suspiciously wondering about his motives.

'I'm not testing you, lad. It's a serious question and if you've never heard of it just say so.' He couldn't have asked a person with stronger views, and I responded immediately.

'It's an opioid that saw the light of day in the early 60s to help addicts come off heroin,' I said. 'In the mid-60s, some boffin – with nothing better to do – decided to do a drug trial on people with alcohol problems to see if it worked for them. I actually applied and was accepted. We got paid well but it turned into a farce.'

'Exactly what do you mean by that?' The Doc was wearing his fascinated expression and so I smiled and continued.

'There were ten of us, if I remember correctly, and two male nurses; one did days and the other nights. Occasionally, we had visitors from a drug company, but in the main we were left alone and allowed to wander around the grounds of what I think may have once been a stately home. The day nurse was ever-present and enjoyed lunchtimes as much as we did; at least for the first couple of weeks. The main reason being there was a private bar which was free and open every day between 12pm and 2pm, and we got systematically pissed every day.

'Then, on Day 15, the medication started and with it the lunchtime atmosphere began to lose its jollity. In simple language, the alcohol lost its effect. I can't remember whether everyone suffered withdrawal but I was one of those who did, and I recall one chap had a seizure, although he recovered okay.

'The purpose of the drug, as far as we could see, was it acted as some sort of neutraliser to the effects of ethanol, which initially it was found to do in the case of heroin. The bloody fools seem to overlook the fact that users of any drug do so for effect, and so the desire to stop has to be at least equal to the desire for the fix. A drug such as Nalorex is pointless in the scheme of things, simply because when the call for any drug fix is loud enough, all the addict will do is stop taking it.

'Later I discovered Nalorex had an active ingredient called Naltrexone, so imagine my reaction when it reappeared under this name some years later; talk about clutching at bloody straws! They just don't get it Doc! What they need to pursue is what I'm doing. Tackle the approach to alcohol abuse from a cultural point of view over time with a tool that has an awareness, advisory, educational and treatment element.'

I loaded my fork with the last piece of sausage and fried bread only to find it was cold, but I enjoyed it just the same.

'So, you don't feel strongly about it then?' The Doc's voice was grim. He looked serious, and then his eyes twinkled as they often did, and finally he burst out laughing. I wasn't sure why at first, but I fell in and laughed too, although I didn't really think it was as funny as he did. What I very much appreciated was that he ordered more coffee and that made me smile.

*

Back at the surgery, we continued our addiction chat and I learned a great deal from another point of view; this included the advice not to be so dogmatic.

'Remember, all points of view have a value,' Dr Weiser advised and I made a mental note to heed the advice; at the same time, I decided to retain at least some of my cynicism.

'Ahhh! Here comes Ken,' the Doc announced as a slightly hunched figure, with his glasses held together with sticking plaster, crossed the road and opened the surgery door.

'Now… I know you two need no introduction.' The Doc looked pleased with himself, 'Ken requested a one-to-one with you Nick and I said you wouldn't mind.' Ken held out a grimy hand, and I shook it readily enough although I was still a shade taken aback.

'Take him through, Nick.' The Doc sounded like he'd already got his mind on his next patient and probably had, so I did as bid and the first thing I saw was my carrier bags nestling between two chairs.

Ken and I settled ourselves down by the cosy cast iron furnace, and after removing our outer coats, settled in a convivial atmosphere of our own making.

'Don't mind me asking, but I was wondering why you wanted to meet up on a one-to-one basis?' Then, I added hastily, 'Not that I mind in the least.'

Ken studied me through his crooked glasses, made so probably because he had tried to repair them without being able to see properly; not many dossers had spare specs!

'It was the story of Bridgmidge,' he began. 'When I was a kid, I went to Sunday school and some of the Bible stories were written for children to understand and they were quite different; I think it reminded me of them.' He looked at me waiting for an answer and so I said the first thing that came into my head.

'The Doc calls them parables. I didn't set out intending them to sound like that; I suppose it has happened that way by chance. Do you think I should try and rewrite them in another style?'

'No bloody way!' Ken's voice turned to annoyance and with it the atmosphere.

'It worked for me. If it hadn't, I wouldn't be here; I'd be sat round the Spitalfields fire necking shit drink or cheap cider at best! I'm here because I want to hear more, and the Doc said you'd got loads.'

'I have…' I reached for the nearest carrier and lifted it onto my lap.

'I haven't planned anything specific, Ken,' I said. 'I hadn't a clue what you wanted to see me about until now, so how about I talk you through the history of them all, and see where it leads? Is that okay?' Ken seemed calmer, nodded and stretched out his hands towards the furnace. The atmosphere was pleasant again.

I grabbed half a dozen pages or so from what I knew was the top of the pile even though they were packed sideways, and was pleased at the outcome. I began to read aloud the notes I had made about my journey so far.

'I used to go to AA meetings out of desperation and also to get out of the cold,' I began. 'One night I met a nice old man called Frank who took pity on me. We'd walk miles to attend different meetings and he'd buy me tea or coffee along the way.'

Abruptly, I found myself in full flow.

'I stayed sober for six months, got a job as a waiter, and made some decent friends… and then the wheels came off. I wandered into a cosily-lit pub that had a log fire, a buzz of happy contented talk and laughter, and I approached the bar to order a glass of lemonade but my teeth were locked together. I stared at the barman helplessly and they only unlocked when I said, 'Double brandy please.'

'No logic there. The following days were lost in a sea of alcohol and blurred faces. There was a fight and I was a victim not a challenger, no strength to retaliate, no reason for me to engage. Accident & Emergency was the next step which led to a hospital bed by way of B&B.

'Word gets round fast in the world of those who drink together and others who have triumphed over its grip. My old friend, Frank from AA, heard the news and came to visit me and we talked endlessly of my folly. Finally, I asked if we could go back to our walks again following my discharge and he agreed, and our first outing had an enormous impact on me.

'He invited me to accompany him on a visit to a hospice for alcohol dependents. It was a sad place, like entering a world of automatons, people walking about like clockwork toys. Others lay in bed not able to move at all. My friend had told me, even before I entered, that all of the occupants were terminally ill with a condition called Wernicke-Korsakoff's Syndrome or WKS, which is a neurological disorder caused largely by alcohol abuse.

'As I looked around me, one thought did cross my mind just for a fleeting second. How close right now was I to this place or somewhere like it? How near am I to a final, sinister point of no return? I knew I was drinking large amounts of alcohol too often. I knew I had drunk too much, too often, too young, and I didn't know for sure the extent of the damage inside my head. The same thoughts may not occur to many, because this and many other conditions are caused by alcohol, and rarely is this accepted or deemed important enough to flag up early warning systems by the medical profession. How many people, for example, know alcohol is a carcinogen – a substance known to cause cancer in living tissue? There are many people in responsible positions who should know better than to let all of this happen without offering some warning into the risks. Yet, the fact remains, they don't and the blame has to lie somewhere! Surely someone *specific* should be given the responsibility, directly, to ensure such information is shared amongst a population that likes to drink?

'I followed my friend to a cot-like bed in a side room where a man lay with eyes staring vacantly at the ceiling. I estimated him to be in his early fifties, and a lady who I assumed was his wife, sat holding his hand. She was introduced to me as Vera and her husband – who lay by her side in the cot with metal sides – was Jim Conway.

'Jim wore a nappy. They had put a nightshirt over it in an attempt to conceal the fact – to protect his modesty and make him look presentable – but it hadn't really worked.

'My friend told me Jim had been financial director of a huge industrial organisation which was situated somewhere on the Thames Embankment, near Lambeth Bridge. He had drunk whisky in profusion without understanding the dangers, which was a terrible tragedy as things turned out. One day, those close to him noticed he had started to forget things. His doctor put him in touch with a neurologist who knew about the work of Professor Korsakoff, a famous Russian neurologist, a brilliant man who discovered brain damage in people who abused alcohol without realising the dangers. Jim was told he had it, but he still kept drinking and now he was in never-never-land and I had come to visit him. Nowadays, Jim could only say: '*Mama, Dada and Vera.*' But as I visited him more frequently, he learned another word… *Nick*… and it became '*Mama, Dada, Vera and Nick.*' But there was a horrifying part yet to come, and I feel a sick feeling whenever I think of it.

'Every now and again, perhaps once or twice a fortnight, he would seem to emerge from his state of dementia just as if he was normal. He would sit up, look around, start to shake and then utter the most unforgettable and haunting words while grabbing his wife Vera's hands.

'Oh! My God, Vera… I know what's happened to me!'

Just as quickly, and perhaps mercifully, he would slip back into his state of dementia and a dreadful silence would linger, as noticeable as the sun slipping behind a cloud.

'Of course, Jim Conway's story didn't begin at the hospice. Neither did it start following a promotion to financial director. He had loved alcohol and its effect for many a long year but was fortunate in one respect – it didn't cause him to be violent or even angry. The truth was, he became more and more amiable as he continued to drink, and yet inexplicably he knew how to stop before offending anyone or appearing to be thoroughly intoxicated.

'Some thought it odd that he frequently disappeared from gatherings fairly late on; none knew he was actually paralytic and some sixth sense deep within his addicted soul gave him sufficient warning to make his escape before he tarnished his reputation.

'The day eventually came, however, when alcohol became the main man. Jim and Vera decided to search for help. AA came and went. An order of nuns in the north of England tried hard, followed by an order of monks in Wales; they were shadowed by a group of well-meaning hippies who had a small farm, on the north Yorkshire moors. The process always ended with Jim back at his local pub pretending to drink non-alcoholic tomato juice, each containing a double whisky. Now, Jim's only friends were Mama, Dada, Vera and Nick.

'He had passed a final point of no return.'

The story had come to an end, and I stopped reading.

Ken shuffled his feet, then got up and walked around the furnace before sitting back down again. He made a few humming sounds, and one or two may have been grunts; then, unexpectedly, he spoke firmly and in a clear voice.

'I'm gonna ask the Doc for a detox and see if I can beat it. Can we meet up again, Nick?'

'Of course,' I replied. 'If you think it will help.' I spoke as confidently as I could make myself sound. Just then there was a knock on the door leading to the surgery, it opened and the Doc entered… followed by Ginger!

'Sorry to interrupt you, gentlemen,' he said in his comforting accent, 'but I would like you both to meet Karen Rigby-Jones.'

11: FUNNY OLD WORLD

It took me several seconds to overcome my surprise. Not because Ginger was a patient of Dr Weiser's, simply the coincidence that was happening. Later, we laughed when she told me my mouth opened and closed several times before I spoke.

'Ginger… err Karen and I are already acquainted, and err… I think you could say we are friends.'

The Doc's eyes scanned us both rapidly, and when no animosity appeared to present itself, he added, 'Jolly good. This may very well solve an immediate problem we have… won't it, Karen?' Ginger lowered her eyes, her pale skin suddenly becoming a delightful pink.

'Well, I've got to go and get my sub from the SS,' Ken had chimed into the conversation, and his voice saved the moment. 'Nick and I are going to do this again if it's okay with you, Doc. And from my point of view the sooner, the better. Oh, and by the way, I would like you to reconsider me for that detox I turned down.' The Doc responded in the affirmative and Ken disappeared into the street.

'Shall we go and sit by the warmth of the fire? It would be a shame to waste it and I'm only going to let it burn out.' The Doc was right; although a large room, it was well insulated despite its corrugated roof and general appearance, and we were soon sat together in the warm.

'What a surprise,' remarked the Doc, the twinkle having returned to his eyes. While I was a shade embarrassed, Ginger was in her element. She described how we met and our evening together, and did a complete detailed rundown of how I had cooked a feast (as she described it), even down to the fact it had been created on a single Baby Belling hotplate. The Doc brought things back to the moment.

'Tell me, which would you prefer to be called? Karen or Ginger?' He focused on her without asking how the nickname had arisen and her reply was immediate.

'New start, new name. Please call me Ginger; I actually quite like it.' She sat looking first at the Doc, then at me, and then back again with her lips pressed firmly together.

Dr Weiser clapped his hands loudly and said, 'Right, that's settled then. Now, how say we ask Nick to be your RA, Ginger?' She looked pensive, and then abruptly I detected a hint of panic and decided to intervene.

'What's an RA, Doc?' I asked him. 'Responsible Adult,' he responded at once. 'Ginger has decided to have a methadone detox and that is why she is here today.' I decided it was time for me to help them both out by joining in with the conversation, and I did so by explaining I at least knew of her plans.

'Ginger said she was going to see about a detox,' I began, 'but I had no idea it was to be with you. Well done, Ginger. I admire you and I will do anything I can to help.' My voice ended on an unintended high, reflecting my enthusiasm and genuine admiration for her decision. 'Tell me what I have to do,' I added almost as an afterthought.

'The Doc stretched his legs out towards the furnace, hands clasped together across his chest and we waited.

'Ginger has been off heroin for several months thanks to a drug called Methadone which was prescribed during a hospital stay. I am in total support with her decision to be weaned off this, too, now she feels ready. The fact is, too many doctors see it as a permanent fixture once the dreaded heroin is out of the picture. This won't be an easy ride, though. Methadone is a powerful synthetic analgesic. So we need to substitute it for Amitriptyline.'

I trawled my mind for what knowledge I had about heroin addiction.

'And do you think she should have some Diazepam as a backup?' I suggested.

The Doc nodded. 'Bingo, good idea, Nick,' he said, before addressing Ginger. 'When do you want to start it?'

'Nick?' she asked, nervously looking at me. Now, the ball was in my court and I didn't hesitate.

'How say tomorrow?'

Ginger agreed and Dr Weiser wrote out a prescription which he handed to me with the words, 'You're in charge now. St Leonards Hospital is your first stop in an emergency; do we understand one another?'

'Yes sir, absobloodylutely,' I answered firmly.

*

Ginger and I visited the nearest pharmacy to arrange her prescription.

'So what do you intend to do now?' I asked as we left.

'I don't want to go back to my place to discuss the detox; I would like to keep my mind occupied elsewhere for as long as I can. Would you mind if we went window-shopping, Nick? We could walk in the direction of Oxford Street.'

Ginger's words had tumbled out quickly and I detected a note of panic.

'You've done this before, haven't you?' I asked, and she nodded furiously as if to emphasise the terrors.

'You won't be alone, Ginger.'

'Neither will you. You know the RA has to stay with me for ten days, 24 hours a day?!'

'Really?' The shock in my voice was pronounced and I stood looking at her in bewilderment. 'But you've only got one room!' Then, with the most innocent of smiles and in her very best public school accent, she replied, 'Do you really think you will be in any danger from me jumping on you in the state I'm going to be in, Nicholas?'

'My mother was the last person to call me that,' I uttered. Ginger could see the bewilderment in my eyes – me, responsible for someone undergoing a detox, and her being out of it, for 10 days! – and I offered a disoriented 'You must think I'm a big kid.' My realisation was underpinned by how sick I had become; the terrifying extent to which alcohol had affected me. Its damage had altered the way I viewed life and normal living; it had left me childlike in many ways.

I wrestled with my inner self in an attempt to rapidly reconcile the situation and the psychological damage I had undergone, but I gave up almost at once. It was never going to happen quickly; I was facing a long job!

I put my arm through Ginger's and fought to put one foot in front of the other and let her guide me while I took little notice of direction. Neither of us spoke and my thoughts wandered back to the detox ahead. First, I felt panic and wished I'd never set out to research and then write the notes which had so impressed Dr Weiser. Then, and maybe thanks to our long walk inducing blood flow and stimulating my thoughts, I began to feel more positive and even optimistic.

I told Ginger of my thoughts, and then about a film called 'Fantastic Voyage'. In it, they miniaturised matter – namely three men, a woman and a submarine – by shrinking individual atoms and allowing them to travel through the human body. I told her it would take a scientific breakthrough such as this to sort out my alcoholic brain. Poor Ginger wasn't in my head; she had problems of her own and hadn't a clue what I was talking about.

*

We approached a musical instrument shop, and I stopped to feast my eyes on the glittering array of guitars, banjos, keyboards, amplifiers and much more professional equipment on display. I was still in a kind of trance, and then abruptly became aware of the sound of Ginger's voice.

'For the third time, do you still miss it?'

'Miss what?' I retorted unkindly.

'Your singing and music career of course.'

'Yes, of course I do; I miss it like hell!'

'Do you think you will ever play again, Nick?'

I didn't want to talk about it and Ginger meant no harm, but her words stung; hardly an hour of any day went by without me fantasising of working on stage again. In reality, I was as far away from performing professionally, as I was from being honoured by Her Majesty the Queen, *'for services to written notes in carrier bags'*.

No money, no job, nowhere to live, and a reputation for unreliability and suspected insanity, all because of my addiction to alcohol. I hadn't done anything resembling a show for as long as I could remember (busking apart), and memories of the embarrassing things I had done flooded back. The contents in the shop window were blurred by my tears and I felt faint…

'C'mon Nick, please!' Ginger led me away at the same time saying, 'You went so pale I thought you were going to pass out. Are you sure you're all right?'

'I'm okay. I gave some of the best years of my life to my musical career and watched it die due to my drinking. I'm not sure if you will understand, but in a way I think a part of me is in mourning!'

We walked and walked and then walked some more, and then shared a cup of coffee. Ginger drank her half and pushed the remainder towards me, but before I had time to pick it up, a Mediterranean-looking waiter arrived at our table and moved it back to her. He then placed a second one in front of me and walked away without a word.

I was moved beyond words and embarrassed in equal measures. This kind man had determined we were impoverished, but for me it was much more; his gesture was a moment of recognition of my personal failure, and a discernment of what I had become. For several weeks, I had been sober and the real me was slowly emerging. However, what I had done to myself had been an almost mechanical process of destruction. I had turned into a drinking machine that, although malfunctioning, refused to come to a halt; it seemed that only death would turn off the power. But, from the very moment the second coffee arrived, something stirred in my conscience, and it told me I should never allow such a charitable act to be necessary in my life, ever again.

'I suppose he did that because we looked pathetic!' My words snapped me out of a state of self-pity, replacing it with determination and aspirations of deliverance with renewed hope. I had occasionally mused despondently, when homeless and sleeping rough, that I had nothing to show for my life on earth. It was through this twisted, alcoholically misguided mindset that I consoled myself with the belief that in the hours of darkness the streets were mine. Now, something had shifted. I could see

Ginger's detox as a milestone and the first in a crusade against formidable odds. The hard part was I had to find permanent sobriety and it had to be soon. I was running out of time! The point of no return beckoned.

*

'How much money have you got left?' Ginger once more interrupted my train of thought, although this time I was pleased.

'Enough to get a bus home,' I said with a manic smile.

'Let's catch one then,' she replied, unaware of the nature of my sudden inspiration. I turned to acknowledge the one-of-a-kind waiter as we left the premises; sadly, he was nowhere to be seen.

I began to think of what was coming up, for I had no experience of methadone withdrawal, which concerned me, but on the way home I decided the Doc would have warned me had there been an element of the unexpected. My judgment was to treat Ginger as an advanced alcoholic trying to kick the habit, which was something I really did understand and – if my hunch was correct – the symptoms would not be worlds apart. Then I remembered my ongoing place at the hostel, and decided I'd better mention my forthcoming absence to them sooner rather than later.

More by luck than judgement, the bus took us all the way to Aldgate, and we stopped at the chemist on our way back to Ginger's bedsit to collect her prescription. Once she was safely installed, I stated officiously, 'My job as RA begins here.' My tone was not unfriendly nor without compassion, but she had to know I was in charge. 'I'm now going to tell the hostel of the Doc's plan and then I'll be straight back,' I said firmly. 'It's not that I don't trust you, but I'm taking the medication with me.' Ginger nodded meekly, then put the kettle on and sat down with a bump.

*

I was delighted to find the Doc had beaten me to it, and the hostel reception knew I was dealing with a patient on his behalf. I seemed to have gone up in the pecking order which exists in such places, judging by a certain note of respect, which was unusual. When the man on reception wished me well with my patient by referring to them as *him*, I knew the Doc had used absolute discretion and I was glad. My new standing remained intact.

I was barely away half an hour, and when I turned my newly acquired key in the lock, it was to find Ginger exactly as I had left her.

It remained for me to make a pot of tea and while it was standing in customary fashion, I examined the medication. 28 x Diazepam 10mg tablets marked *as prescribed* which effectively left it up to me. A cardboard box labelled 40 x 25mg Amitriptyline tablets, and a further one labelled 40 x 50mg Amitriptyline tablets; both stated ten days supply on the labels. A separate note stipulated no more than 4 x 50mg in the first 24 hours, clearly leaving the reduction plan to me. A further reference advised that Ginger's methadone dose had been suspended.

I paused for a moment to consider how barmy my situation appeared. All the indications were that Dr Weiser had based my credentials on the carrier bag notes; he had decided I knew how detoxification reduction worked across the board, and I hoped he was right. I also felt an acute responsibility for every word I had written in my carrier bags. However, I decided there and then to check and double-check every page as I typed them out from this moment onwards.

I was not in the least concerned by being challenged in regard to my findings, opinions, and views on the subject of alcohol addiction, and I would fight my corner with anyone. Just the same, the Doc's faith and belief in me and my written word meant he was putting his head on the line. I wondered what the reaction of the General Medical Council might be in the event of a death, if he produced – in evidence – a scruffy dosser and two plastic bags so battered the supermarket names had faded away! But, hey, The Doc believed in me and this was my first taste of duty, onus, obligation – in fact total responsibility – and abruptly I tasted fear of the most appalling kind! Out loud, I spoke casually.

'I never thought to ask you Ginger, but have you had your methadone today?' I looked at her expectantly and she shook her head.

'Does the Doc know that?' She shook her head again. 'I have to take it at the pharmacy under supervision; it was the last day today and I told them I didn't want it.'

'Why on earth did you do that?'

'A gesture of intent,' she countered.

Her public school accent was back in evidence, not that it ever really left her, but she seemed to do her best to trim it short of the ridicule which was inevitable from those she mixed with, in and around the demolition-battered East End.

For the first time, I noticed a bulky sleeping bag lying alongside a wall where a radiator was situated, and Ginger noticed it had drawn my attention.

'I thought you might be more at ease, Nick, and in any case, I'm going to have a very restless night… I'm certain of that.' I was a tad ashamed as my childlike state reared its head once more, but grateful all the same. She wouldn't know I had no intention of doing anything other than lie awake listening to her breathing, just to make sure she did!

It was now early evening, and although I had no way of knowing definitively how Ginger would react to her methadone detox, she had described her various attempts at the heroin variety as horrendous. My best guess was we were in for a rocky ride. I had given things a great deal of thought and was about to put part of my plan to her.

'I want you to trust me, Ginger. I know we have walked a lot today, but I need you to agree to my suggestion of yet another walk. Believe me, the more exhausted you are, the more bearable it's going to be.' At first, she didn't appear to have the will to argue and I wondered if it was the right decision, then I snapped out of it and insisted firmly, 'I think we should walk to London Bridge and back. It can do no harm.'

'Whaaaat…? That must be five bloody miles,' she protested.

'Just short of six there and back,' I retorted with a smile, 'C'mon it'll do us both good, I added, making sure I had the Diazepam in my pocket and grabbing a small bottle of water from the side of her bed. Her face was a picture as she dragged her coat back on and half-stumbled out through the door leaving me behind to lock it.

Ginger was conspicuous by her silence and began making tuneless humming noises. After a while, I stopped by a bench, sat her down, and gave her half a 10mg Diazepam tablet, and then allowed her five minutes for it to begin working while she sipped water from the bottle.

'Tell me more about your family and where you grew up?' She showed an atom of interest and so I took heart and joined in with more questions, and soon we were stood looking over the balustrade at London Bridge. I suggested going further to Borough High Street, but Ginger's pained expression told me it best to head home and so we did. I hoped the walk would prove to be beneficial.

The moment we arrived back at the bedsit, Ginger, now quite exhausted, decided to go straight to bed. I offered to go outside while she undressed, but she pointed to the bathroom and, without a word, wobbled towards it, her nightclothes under an arm. By the time she reappeared, I was in the sleeping bag, hands linked behind my head, looking in her direction and having already put the medication away safely. I directed her to a 25mg tablet of Amitriptyline on her bedside table next to a glass of water; she swallowed it immediately and disappeared under the clothes without a word.

The room was hushed. I lay on the carpeted floor in one of the most comfortable sleeping bags I had ever encountered and stared at the reposed – soon to be tormented – sleeping form just a few feet away. Ginger's peace was almost certain to be temporary, and I wondered how long it would last. I had no experience of narcotic detox, and although this aspect had already been reduced by the introduction of Methadone, I had heard addicts on the streets describe flashbacks months after successful detoxes.

I turned sideways to check the time on a tiny travel clock with bright luminous hands. It was almost 2am, and I suddenly realised I'd dozed off. I sat up, my eyes straining, aided only by a shaft of street light allowed into the bedsit through a transom window above the street door. Ginger was sleeping easily, her breathing was even, and her face was slightly illuminated; she looked more like her twenty-four years than she did when she was awake.

I must have dozed off again because I was awakened abruptly by the alarming sound of Ginger having a violent nightmare. I was out of the sleeping bag and on my feet in seconds. She was tossing, turning, and shouting indecipherable words hysterically. I thought it inevitable she would wake herself up, then unexpectedly her ravings abated and she lay still, her breathing steady once more. I realised I had taken in a deep breath and was holding it perhaps in trepidation, before necessity forced me to expel it with a sound resembling a mighty rushing wind!

Almost four hours passed, during which I remained awake. I had given up trying to read, unable to find anything that interested me, and I had refrained from too much movement for fear of waking Ginger. The small table lamp on the floor beside me wasn't at all bright, but just the same I turned it off for the same reason.

I lay there thinking about my life and wondering where events were taking me. I believed in God, but I was convinced the hurt my drinking had brought upon others – particularly the worry and despair I had heaped on my poor mother – was unforgivable. Then Ginger woke up.

'Nick! Nick! Where are you?' I switched on the light. Although it was a low watt bulb, it dazzled both of us momentarily, and its glow emphasised her pale face. The clock that glowed in the darkness said 6am.

'I'm here, don't worry. I'll make some tea, but first you must have some medication.' I reached for a further 25mg Amitriptyline tablet, gave it to her with a glass of water and then filled the kettle and switched it on.

'How do you feel right now?'

'I'm pretty bad Nick, I want to be sick but I can't. I'm sweating like a pig, too.'

I knew some of the detox drugs caused sickness and this created problems if they didn't stay down long enough to get into the bloodstream. This would definitely be a cause for worry.

'Do your best not to be sick. We must try to keep the medication down or the withdrawal symptoms will continue,' I told her. Then I remembered about a sickness reliever passed down from a previous generation.

'Have you got any bicarbonate of soda?' I asked.

'In the left-hand side cupboard, top shelf,' she replied. I found it at once and put half a teaspoon into a small amount of water.

'Drink this slowly,' I ordered. She did so and soon afterwards announced the sick feeling had gone, and I sighed with relief.

We drank the tea and I tried hard to introduce some idle chat to distract her from the discomforts of the moment.

'Tell me about your mum and dad.' It was the first thing that came into my head and she looked at me oddly.

'I *have* told you bits.' Her words sounded like a protest.

'Not really,' I answered quickly. 'Not that much.' Ginger reflected, as though carefully choosing her words, and when she did reply, she sounded wistful.

'Daddy plays the organ… badly, although I would never tell him so, and Mum is gardening mad. They both love to go and see live nostalgia shows, especially musicals.

'Mummy and Daddy are…! err…! were…' now she stumbled over her words, and small sobs were emitted as she completed her sentence, '…were lovely people. I'm an only child and we really loved each other. And I don't know whether they are alive or dead.'

'And they don't know if you're alive or dead either?'

Ginger sobbed even more, wiping her eyes on a screwed-up tissue and I considered what a mess I was making of taking her mind off her detox suffering. Nevertheless, we talked on, and finally she lapsed into another fitful sleep.

An hour passed and then the nightmares or perhaps hallucinations began again and ran their course. I left the light switched on, then took a chance and popped two doors along to where I'd spotted a newsagent. I returned quickly and was about to settle down for a quiet read of the morning paper when another episode kicked off. I sat on the side of her bed and looked down, trying to imagine the torment that was going on in her mind, although I had a pretty good idea. We were all different, no doubt, but some of my withdrawal experiences were very real and seemed to run and run. The brain, eh? A complex piece of human machinery much more sophisticated than any computer, yet unpredictable and indefinable. Ginger's face was contorted by an ugly grimace and her head thrashed from side to side, red hair soaked straight, shapeless, and darkly discoloured by sweat.

I went to the bathroom and grabbed a couple of hand towels and did my best to dry her hair, face and neck, but it was a losing battle. Then I tried a cold compress using a face flannel, refreshing it from a bowl of cold water and this time I had better luck. The next task was to keep her warm. She kept kicking her bedclothes off, and my only option was to keep replacing them until the violence in her tortured psyche had run its course.

Just as the winter daylight emerged, replacing the shaft of nighttime street illumination, Ginger sat bolt upright as if charged by electricity. A shocking scream filled the flat and I was by her side. She was shaking uncontrollably, perspiration soaking her face. With difficulty, I managed to wake her and administered 10mg of Diazepam. Slowly, her tenseness and rigidity relaxed, and she seemed to sink into the mattress. I had an overcoat of sorts which was hung behind the door and I placed it over the counterpane, in an effort to maintain her body temperature.

'I'll get you for this, you bastard! Breaking into my home, I'm not going back with you, I'd rather die!' There was no endearment in any of her words, but neither was there any sense or reason. They were delivered, not in the vicious salvo they may have implied, but in a sad and pathetic whisper as the madness receded. Ginger was delirious, her mind outraged by serious withdrawal symptoms. With difficulty, I administered a further 10mg of Diazepam.

I was as sure as I possibly could be that she probably needed more Amitriptyline in her system, but I was mindful of the Doc's instructions. Then I was overcome by the logic of my years of experience involving others as well as myself. I suspected she may have vomited up some of the previous dose of

Amitriptyline when I was asleep, which was why she was suffering so much. Now she was nearly due her next dose. I crushed up a 25mg tablet, made a pot of tea and poured a cup for Ginger, carefully stirring in the powder. I hoped this would get into her system more quickly.

Ginger's eyes were closed, her breathing uneven, and she was still perspiring freely. I propped her up with pillows against the headboard with some difficulty, stirred the tea until it was cool, and with a minimum of force did my best to get her to drink it. I estimated at least half ended up in the bed or on her cotton top, and so I repeated the process and had better luck second time around. I now lived in hope she'd had enough to compensate any loss.

I must have been desperately tired, because the next thing I knew I was awake and the tiny friendly clock told me it was mid-afternoon. Remembering Ginger's plight, and my attempts to help her, I was by her side immediately; she was still. For a split second, I thought she was dead. I leant over her body and when I detected she was breathing evenly and peacefully I fell to my knees in prayer.

For the first time since my studies into alcohol addiction had begun, the reality of the burden of *responsibility* which accompanied my carrier bags full of notes, hit me like a hammer blow. In my moment of panic, the power of having to make decisions, the results of which could determine life and death, cast a giant shadow over my hopes, dreams, and endeavours.

Yet in those milliseconds, I experienced a hardening of my resolve and words without a voice entered my head saying alcohol was doing more harm than I could ever do. Nevertheless, I vowed this would be my first and last narcotic-related detox.

*

'Coffee please… strong,' said Ginger before pointing towards the bathroom and I helped her negotiate the few feet towards it, closing the door for privacy but telling her not to lock it. By the time she returned, two mugs of coffee were in place and we both supped noisily.

'I bet they don't make noises like this when they drink coffee at the Sorbonne,' I remarked casually but with a smile. There was a short silence before she replied.

'I didn't get the chance to find out,' was her only comment.

Over the course of the day, I administered 25mg of Amitriptyline four times, told her so, and informed her I was counting the extra milligrams she'd had so far. I had determined there was a possibility she was over the worst and told her so. All she did was nod, and I gave her the second *official* dose which she swallowed at once.

We then both took turns to shower and brush our teeth.

'I'm not sure I really wanted to go there,' she said afterwards, and I waited for her to qualify her statement but she did not. I waited for what seemed an appropriate period of time and then decided to enquire politely.

'Go where?' I asked and then for some reason expected to be admonished for not following the conversation; instead, she answered simply, 'The Sorbonne.'

Less than half an hour later, we were walking once more towards the river at London Bridge. There was little conversation between us, mainly rudimental stuff and aimless comments, and then it changed.

'I had some terrible nightmares, Nick. In one, I went back on heroin and I woke up wanting a fix, and the craving was the worst imaginable. I still feel like one now, but it's not as bad as it was, and I swear to God I won't! Honestly, I feel much more able to fight it right now. The Doc was right, having you there made all the difference.'

I felt so much better hearing her talk this way, and thanked the heavens above she had been through the heroin detox before I had met her. Although I had suggested otherwise, if the night before was anything to go by, there was little chance she would make a rapid recovery from the methadone detoxification. It would be a complex road, and Ginger would be under sufferance and temptation for a long time to come. Abruptly, her voice interrupted my thoughts.

'Another of the nightmares was finding myself on my own,' she said, her voice at fever pitch. 'You had gone and left me. I was alone in a room full of crazy people all shooting up… You won't leave me, will you, Nick?'

She was undoubtedly confused and unsure of the difference between actuality and delusion. I had no wish to make matters worse and promised, without hesitation, that I would not be leaving her under any circumstances.

*

As the days passed, Ginger continued to suffer and endure, but there was no repeat of the savagery of the first night, and it was no longer necessary for me to lie awake hour after hour. Nonetheless, on successive nights she sweated and cried in mental agony, and I played the numbers game with the medication, determined by each episode as they presented themselves. Time and time again, I woke and had to force myself into full consciousness, believing she had called out, only to find there was no war and she was fast asleep, and there was no battle to fight.

This pattern repeated itself day after day, but noticeable improvements took place towards the end of the second week. I had long given up on any ideas of adopting the ten-day reducing programme which worked so well for people with alcohol problems; the two procedures were worlds apart. Instead, I literally handed out the medication when I estimated the need demanded it, which was often at first, but in the scheme of things only extended the process by four days.

I had telephoned the Doc at the halfway stage, but spared him the violent descriptions of her trauma, although in the weeks that followed, I did tell him, and he said he had guessed.

Stability kicked in during the third week, and by the fourth, the utterly charming, pragmatic, and eloquent privately-educated Karen Rigby-Jones, emerged in style and in triumph.

*

I had finally presented her to the Doc at the commencement of her third week drug-free and he had tears in his eyes. He hugged both of us jointly and severally many times in the hour we spent with him, and I promised to continue with my Saturday lectures.

As the weeks passed, we spent more and more time with him, and one day, a battered typewriter caught Ginger's eye. The outcome of this was she offered to type out the results of my editing which had become a daily task.

Dr Weiser was pleased to have us both working with him at his surgery although Ginger insisted on some changes. She swept, cleaned, and washed surfaces and then insisted he bought some Magnolia wall paint, having discovered I was a dab hand with a brush. Life had taken on another dimension for all of us, and in particular for me. Eight weeks after I had met Ginger at the all-night caravan eating place, we became an item, and I took up residence at her bedsit.

Ginger enjoyed early starts at the Doc's surgery, and as I hated mornings, I followed a couple of hours later. On one such day, she had just left when I spotted an empty envelope on an ornamental shelf which had a village address on it I had never heard of. A quick look at an Atlas at the newsagents next door told me it was north of the Yorkshire Dales which she had once mentioned. I knew it had to be her parents' address and an idea came to me.

I was full of admiration for Ginger's achievement, and suddenly felt compelled to let them know their lovely daughter was alive and well in the hope they could be reunited. It was a crazy notion, and I knew there were risks, but she often spoke of them lovingly and I thought I knew her well enough to take the chance. I wrote a couple of pages telling them of her deliverance from addiction and how their daughter was a beautiful young woman. Then I posted it on the way to the Doc's surgery, and promptly forgot all about it.

*

As much as Ginger's sobriety progress was inspiring in its apparent totality, mine was another matter. Although I hadn't been counting (which, in itself, was unusual given previous attempts) I estimated that I had not used alcohol in three months. The odd thing was that I lived with an ever-present contemplation that resided in my brain, which was how I would face the Doc after my next boozy session.

For close on four years, I had been writing about alcoholic lives amongst the homeless population, and recording their horrors at the hands of their addiction. I'd spent many a long hour researching and studying in libraries, and I'd even gone to the lengths of devising a questionnaire of sorts. This I used without shame or embarrassment, spending hours approaching members of the public at Liverpool Street Station enquiring of their drinking habits. The majority brushed me aside, although the number who seemed only too pleased to open up and ask questions of me and my motives was surprising. Many departed, saying they would watch their alcohol intake in the future. Yet here I was, armed with extensive knowledge and opinion in abundance, receiving praise galore from a doctor who could easily stake a claim to be a leader in the field, while all the time, planning my next drink.

A dilemma I faced – which my muddled mind construed as paramount – was how Ginger would take it if I imbibed. I felt it was this, in the main, which had prevented me from allowing our personal relationship to flourish, and I had interpreted it as *not* being in love with her. Despite us now being an item, I was still unsure of the *being in love* aspect, and I had shared my worries with the Doc. I could see how saddened he was to hear of my doubts, but accepted I was considering Ginger too. Nevertheless, he assured me love would grow alongside compatibility, and he was quite sure we had that in abundance. I deliberated long and hard on a statement I had heard a thousand times when alcohol victims referred to their affair with *Madam Alcohol*. Was my love for her stronger than my commitment to Ginger? In reality, *Madam Alcohol* was the lover of millions of both sexes. How could I defeat her when so many had failed? I knew full well that she, and she alone, was the perpetrator of more murders than could ever be counted. How could this love exist when I knew she was a whore of such monstrous proportions?

Little wonder an alcoholic priest once described to me the long road back from alcohol addiction by citing words spoken by the Prince of Preachers C H Spurgeon, but out of context. He told me to be prepared for a violent voyage, and quoted, 'It was by perseverance, after all, that the snail reached the Ark'. That night we had an early tea and went to the cinema where 'Kelly's

Heroes' was the main feature. I liked a good war film and enjoyed this one enormously, made more so by Ginger liking it too. On the way home, she was in very high spirits and happier than I'd ever seen her, and as we crossed London Bridge she pulled up sharply, pointing high into the sky.

'Look at the stars and that beautiful moon!' We stood together, hand in hand, gazing at the heavens. It was one of those sharp, clear nights when so many stars are visible there seems hardly room to separate them, and then she broke the spell.

'As long as I've got you, Nick, I'll never go back on drugs. I just know it.' Her statement stabbed like a knife; she was unaware of my thoughts and I concentrated on the moon, and so I shall never know if she was looking at me or the stars at that precise moment.

Arriving back at the bedsit, I announced I fancied a long soak in the bath and when I came out of the bathroom, she was in bed with the light out. I crept silently into the space next to her and lay still, knowing somehow I had to try to explain to her that I was powerless when alcohol called my name.

The next thing I knew it was daylight. Ginger was still asleep and someone was knocking on the door. I wobbled towards it only half-awake, struggled with the key, and finally got it open.

'Hello, are you Nick?' I nodded at a smartly dressed middle-aged woman who was smiling at me enquiringly.

'Yes, I am,' I replied, not knowing quite what else to say in my sleepy state.

'How lovely to meet you,' her words sounded irrational given the circumstances, but her voice was soft and cultured. She held out her hand in the traditional offer of greeting and I took it.

'I'm Joy Rigby-Jones,' she announced. 'Karen's mother.'

12: GRAND REUNIONS

My hand went to my mouth, and from behind it, I silently mouthed the words, 'Oh my dear God, this is where all hell breaks loose…!'

Too many thoughts raced too quickly through my mind to be able to concentrate on any of them for long. Why hadn't I told Ginger what I'd done? Do something, you damn fool; don't stand there like the gormless idiot you must look! What do I say to her? You have to say something! She looks like royalty, for Christ's sake!

A crashing sound made me turn around, and Ginger stood behind me deathly pale, broken shards of glass scattered at her feet and an expression of incredulity on her face. A man in a bowler hat I had approached for a handout at Liverpool Street Station had once called me a retard, incapable of dealing with life. Now I knew what he meant. Mental degeneration due to alcohol abuse had robbed me of the ability to react to anguish, or then again there was just a chance it may have been shock!

I shut my eyes, held my breath, and suffered seconds of hell. Then they were in each other's arms, crying and sobbing out each other's names, and I sank into a chair, grateful for the outcome I had hoped and prayed for.

Unexpectedly, the image of a powerfully-built man wreathed in smiles emerged into my consciousness, and stupidly I looked towards the door, wondering where he had come from, half-expecting others to follow. I remained lost for words and a useless bystander.

Then, without warning, the attention was on me. Ginger was still crying, although less hysterically, but Mrs Rigby-Jones was hugging me and the man – who my returning composure deduced must be her father – was shaking my hand. From out of the mayhem, words were beginning to register. Both of them were thanking me for the miracle I had performed, and simultaneously I was struggling to explain I had done little or nothing.

It seemed they believed I alone had returned their long thought dead daughter, safely and in rude health. As I recovered from the shock of opening the door to them, and with my confidence returning, I tried desperately to explain Ginger had helped me as much as I had helped her because I too had a problem. I soon realised I was fighting a losing battle, and decided instead to change the subject and offer them a cup of tea.

The offer was accepted, and it introduced a degree of calm, although – understandably – hugs and kisses interrupted from time to time. I offered to leave and allow them some family time together, the reaction to which was one of horror.

'I think it damn rude of us not to have already welcomed you into the family, lad!' Mr Rigby-Jones' voice, in contrast to that of his wife and daughter, was broad Yorkshire and I warmed to him.

'I was born Jones; she was a Rigby,' he offered by way of introduction. 'She insisted we put them together. The Rigby's are a toffee-nosed lot, but I have to admit it looks good on the lorries and has definitely helped business. I mean, who would you rather entrust hundreds of thousands of pounds worth of stuff you'd manufactured to, a bloke called Sid Jones or Sidney Rigby-Jones?' He laughed heartily, and we all laughed with him.

We spent a further hour or so talking about everything and nothing, and then Joy revealed that high on their agenda was to meet Dr Weiser, who I had mentioned with considerable reverence in my letter.

'Gosh, I completely forgot! he'll wonder what has happened to us!' Ginger sounded alarmed. 'You see, Nick is writing a book which the Doc places great value in. Most of it is in longhand. I volunteered to type it out and I've been doing it at his surgery.'

'I'm not sure it will be a book…' I began, but she interrupted me irritably.

'This is no time to be modest, Nick; we need to get to the surgery as soon as we can so he can see we're okay.'

Ginger got herself ready speedily while I filled in her parents with the Doc's work amongst street people. Before long, we were on our way. There was only one free parking place near to the bedsit, and Sid had been fortunate enough to find it unoccupied; I knew his elegant Jaguar would be safe there till at least 6pm.

*

If they thought the Doc's premises lowly, Ginger's parents showed no sign of it, and Ginger gave them a conducted tour of what we now jokingly called the conference room. The Doc described Ginger as the perfect patient and a most excellent secretary, and when it came to me, he told them I had the capability to become the first-ever Alcohol Consultant.

'I didn't know there was such a thing,' Joy responded in awe.

'There isn't; at least not yet,' he replied mysteriously.

'If I can persuade these two young people to agree, Dr Weiser,' Sid's words changed the subject and his voice immediately grabbed attention, 'Do you think you could spare them for a couple of weeks while they come and stay with us at 'Castle Keep'… err, that's the name of our humble home.' His suggestion came as a complete surprise, and the silence lasted until Ginger's voice saved the situation from becoming awkward.

'Please say yes, Doc,' she begged, pretending his powers extended much further than they did in truth. He played the game and responded gallantly.

'I think you both deserve a holiday. It is well earned and you go with my blessing.' A babble of excitement followed, and only the Doc noticed my reluctance. I was fighting a battle on several fronts, and as all fighters of war knew only too well, more than one front was one too many. I had a beautiful girl wanting me to pledge to her a lifetime of allegiance, and her seemingly enchanting family wanting to adopt me forever. The Doc wanted me as an ally, and in order to follow my dream, I needed him probably more than he needed me. Then there was my lover in a bottle who, if I let out, would destroy my image in a heartbeat, and the chances of me defeating her advances were next to nil. It was only a matter of time before I received the call of the wild!

It was assumed I was as happy with the arrangement as Ginger clearly was, and it would have been churlish to have refused. For once, I considered the realities. At present, I was living in her flat with the alternatives being a dormitory with fifty-plus others, or a city bench, or in a doorway. In practical terms, my hopes for the future lay crumpled in two carrier bags, despite the high hopes the Doc had for them. My stiflingly secret wish – indeed desire – was to be able to drink alcohol like normal people; even though I had proved a thousand times I could not. I knew, for sure, that everyone's personality changed in drink – one way or another – ranging from major to minor, so no one remained their real self once they had imbibed. By definition, they were no longer normal, and this included me, bigtime! In addition, I fervently believed every single person on the planet who consumed the stuff was dependent on it in degrees, which varied similarly. Yet despite all of this, I was secretly committed to finding a way where I could take it or leave it. Confusion in my head reigned supreme.

*

During one Saturday night talk at the Doc's surgery meeting, I stated that unless we could rid the English language of the word *alcoholism*, we would never make a breakthrough in people's perception of the disease. It draws a line in the sand no one wants to cross, and they will deny having done so even at the cost of their own lives. Alcohol users will never be at ease as long as there is such a thing as alcoholism. With its abolition, the replacement phrase – *degrees of dependency* – will not only sound less threatening, it will form a basis for negotiation. As long as there is a boundary labelled as *alcoholism* (plus its social stigma), we will never be able to treat the condition of total dependency.

I remember closing my very first talk, that day in the Doc's office, by reminding the audience that regular users should always be seen as dependents, and that if we are to achieve the all-important objective of managing their alcohol dependency, we must never call them alcoholics, not even in secret.

So much happened in the next hour that I was in a complete whirl. Sid suggested we leave straight away. He pointed out there was nothing to keep us overnight in London, and it would save them the trouble of booking into a hotel. He added how much fun it would be to chat on the journey.

Ginger and I both felt embarrassed as we gathered together our meagre belongings, but it didn't seem to worry her parents, and soon we were on our way north in the luxurious Jaguar.

It was a pleasant journey, and we arrived in the early hours at their village home, north of the Yorkshire Dales. We had been travelling through dark countryside where there was little to see other than atmospheric movie-type clips that the Jaguar's powerful headlights picked out. Unexpectedly, Sid indicated to turn right as he negotiated a turn for no reason other than good driving habit, then we stopped with twenty-foot-high iron gates barring our way. He pressed a button on the dashboard and the huge obstruction slid open, 'A bloke called Giuseppe Manini invented these, you know,' he offered. 'Word is he was obsessed by people who opened the gates to his driveway and then failed to close them; this meant he could do so remotely.'

At night, it was hard to tell how much land the house occupied, although the building itself, while smaller than a full-blown mansion, was substantial indeed. It would be daylight before I would see a garden, landscaped to perfection, with a stream running through the middle. Nevertheless, the car's headlights swept the area as Sid circled a garden island to pull up by the front door, picking out beautifully arranged shrubs and flower beds surrounding a lawn that would have done credit to any bowling club. Sid's voice sounded again, and it was to be the first time his daughter's absence had been referred to.

'There's a white-fenced paddock and stables over there,' he pointed a finger into the darkness, 'and a swimming pool to the right. Beyond are green fields which stretch to the edges of woodland. Karen used to play there for hours when she was a little girl. By the way, Karrie…' it was the first time I had heard the abbreviation, and it sounded caring, loving even, yet it was the break in his voice that I noticed, and I wondered if Ginger had too. Sid's voice cut short my conjecture, '…we've looked after Bruno for you, my dear, although he's five years older, of course. But only Mummy has ridden him since you left…' His voice tailed off, and because my thoughts of the hurt alcohol had forced me to leave in my wake were constant, I knew exactly how Ginger felt in that moment. Once more, Sid interrupted my thoughts and perhaps hers too.

'I expect you two will want some time to yourselves,' he said to his wife and daughter, 'so I'll show Nick around the house, so he knows where everything is.' They agreed and departed into the vast kitchen area.

The house itself was a modern, six-bedroomed building in red brick, which I discovered had been built only twenty years before. Immediately inside the front door was a spacious hallway leading to a wide, spiral staircase. The downstairs rooms consisted of a magnificent lounge, capacious dining room, large study and superbly-fitted kitchen. The last room, before negotiating the stairs, was the library, and I wondered inanely if the design was to make it handy for a book at bedtime! Every surface was liberally adorned with expensive-looking ornaments in cut glass, china, and various metals I deduced were brass, copper, silver and gold; the effect was awesome.

I followed Sid up the spiral staircase, and at the top he pushed open a door to reveal a typical teenage girl's bedroom, complete with wall posters, but of a long-gone era. It was a time capsule of memories for a loving mother and father who had done no wrong. 'This was Karrie's room,' he said sadly. 'I don't mean to be morbid, but we left it as she left it, if you can understand that. We hoped and prayed she would come back and we attended morning Mass the day your letter arrived, full of emotion, and thanked God for answering our prayers. There wasn't one scheduled, but the priest is a friend of the family, and he was only too pleased to oblige. I cried for a whole day, had to take it off work, couldn't let the staff see me like that. When I went in the following day, all those who remembered Karrie growing up cried at the sight of me, and it started me off again, so I'd had the day off for nothing.' There was a silence which lasted, and then as calmly as I could, I said, 'I'll tell you what I know if you wish.'

He studied me hard, and then spoke in a whisper. 'In a discreet moment, the Doc told me you were a wise man in the making, held back only by drink. May I ask the sober man, if you think it would help her mother and me, if we could know what happened to Karrie?'

I sat down on a corner of the seventeen-year-old Ginger's bed, and in my imagination searched through my mental carrier bags for the most difficult words to come out of them thus far.

'Karen became a heroin addict through no fault of her own.' Sid gasped and sat down too. I paused intentionally to allow him time to fully absorb the information, and then I continued.

'In many ways, you will find Karen is still seventeen in her behavioural patterns. If she remains drug-free, she will mature slowly but surely, and probably considerably more quickly than you may imagine. My advice is to allow her to do so, and let her tell you what she wants you to know, when she wants you to know it. Your joy will be in the privilege of having your daughter back. Settle for that, Sid. I've spent a lot of time learning from the experiences of others. In terms of addiction, I ask you to consider the following words, *Be advised by the wisest of men, who sought out the wisest of men, to make wiser the wisest of men.*'

He contemplated the phrase while staring at a framed photograph of his daughter on a bedside table, then got up to leave. I held his arm, preventing him from doing so, and said as gently as I could, 'There's something I need to tell you, Sid.'

The fear in his eyes was unmistakable. I still had hold of his arm, and so I squeezed it reassuringly instead of using it to hold him back.

'This will be hard for both of us,' I said, and began wishing I had a stiff brandy, 'but I want you to hear me out and try hard to understand. I haven't finished drinking! Despite having lost everything I hold dear and knowing full well alcohol is my worst enemy, I am more in love with it than I could ever be with Karrie.

'I tell a true story in my lectures for the Doc, about a woman who was gifted a beautiful home but was unable to adjust to normal life and living. Each night she left it, preferring to sleep in squalor with a bottle of surgical spirits. I call it the call of the wild. It is as unimaginable as it is incomprehensible, and I carry it like a cross of agony and anguish every day of my life.'

Sid went to speak, but I stopped him with the flat of my hand and continued. 'Imagine the stink of wretchedness and decay and then try to envisage it as being the perfume of Elysium. Imagine a place where – despite the worst of winter conditions – there is a glow of warmth and comfort, and there you have hell on earth; the favourite living place of the alcoholic vagrant!'

'My dearest, dearest, boy…!' Sid embraced me, and his arms were holding me so tightly I could barely breathe, 'I don't care what it costs me, I will pay for the best treatment there is and we will beat this bloody thing together, this I swear!'

I prised myself loose and turned towards his tear-stained face so he had to look straight at me. 'Sid, there is no one out there in the halls of professional treatment who can help people like me. Medical students, at whatever level, are not taught anything remotely useful in the treatment of alcohol addiction. It is more likely they will *learn* how to drink at university!

'When my work is complete, I hope to have the infrastructure of an early warning system. Instead of lives tragically lost, we will have a way to offer awareness, case studies, actions, and deterrents, or parables as the Doc calls them. I am getting wiser with every page I write and with every day I live… and I believe fervently it is my destiny.'

I paused for a moment. 'In the meantime, I would like to stay with you for a short while, and then leave when I hear the call of the wild. I will not drink in front of your daughter, because it would break her heart to witness the terrible destruction and may even lead her back to heroin. I want her to remember me as I am now. When the time comes, you will have to trust me to deal with Karrie my way, and in the meantime, let's enjoy our time together and love one another.'

Sid sobbed successive sobs, and then seemed to rally, drying his eyes with a tissue from a box on the bedside table that was five years old.

We left Ginger's room and its memories behind us as Sid closed the door; he seemed to force his mood from the misery of the past and present and his voice took on an optimistic note. He pushed open a door and took me into another of the six bedrooms; it was immaculate in every way – a double bedroom with a four-poster bed.

'Joy and I have put you and Karrie in here during your stay.' I had already anticipated this event as inevitable, after all, I had opened the door to Joy in what served as nightclothes and their daughter was still in bed in a single bedsit. It was hardly conducive with a platonic friendship, and they had been perfectly accepting of what would have seemed obvious to anyone.

Neither of us was fully recovered by any standards. The reality of Ginger's mental and physical condition would take time to resume to a normal level of existence, and all of my natural instincts were screwed up beyond normal understanding. Ginger and I were close, of course, but it had only recently moved to another level, and in that moment I decided to add no more and allow the future to take care of itself… even if it didn't take care of me.

Sid had not noticed my trepidation, and it suited me at least for the time being, and we descended the spiral staircase together in pleasant conversation. We rejoined Joy and Ginger, where they now sat in the spacious lounge, and Sid polished off his cup of tea in rapid fashion, as did I. Then, he announced he was going to retire to bed.

'You lot can please yourselves with whatever you want to do,' he said briskly, 'but I'm going to bed. I'm pretty tired after a five hundred mile plus round trip, so I'll see you all in the morning.' Sid gave Ginger a special hug and squeezed both my shoulders warmly while looking me full in the face, and then he was gone. Joy held Ginger tightly as though she was never going to let her go, and when she did, she turned to me and held me long and hard too. Then she whispered in my ear, 'Thank you, my darling, I shall never ever be able to repay you.' Such was her sincerity, I was too choked by the emotion of the moment to find words to argue the small part I had played. And then she left the room, turning only to blow us both a kiss.

Several minutes passed before Ginger and I followed her up the spiral staircase, during which little was said. She pushed open the door to the room that contained the four-poster bed, and I suddenly realised us sharing it had been decided upon at the highest level.

'Did you tell them we are living together; err, I mean as man and wife?' A wicked glint came into Ginger's eyes as she looked straight at me, just as her father had done moments before.

'We might as well live for the moment, Nick.' Her words hung in the air as she placed both arms around me, linking them behind my neck. There was not even the slightest flicker of an eyelash and I stared, perhaps mesmerised for a full thirty seconds. Her eyes were a stunningly clear green, the whites flawless, the lashes long. Her skin seemed unblemished despite pale freckles, which I had noticed were only apparent when she was free of make-up. It was impossible to detect any sign of the ordeal she had been through, and for my part, the call of the wild was silent, still, and but a distant memory.

In that inexpressible moment, she appeared as lovely as any woman could be. I touched her hair, it was soft and as I straightened a curl, it sprang obediently back into place. I was aware of an expensive perfume and felt the warmth of her body against my legs. My hand tightened on her shoulder and then she was in my arms – torment, affliction, plight and ordeal banished in one glorious moment. We clung together without words and it remained that way until dawn broke lazily through a window which should have been curtained but was not… overlooked due to the passion of the night before.

'It's after nine o'clock!' Ginger sounded as if it mattered, but any such thought was quickly alleviated when a knock on the door revealed Joy in her dressing gown, holding a tray of tea and toast.

'I'm so sorry, we slept over,' she showed genuine concern until I informed her we had only just woken up too, and felt it was us who should apologise. Then we all laughed together as Sid appeared over her shoulder.

'Have you two any plans for this evening?' he asked.

*

'There's a concert on at the Garden Theatre tonight,' explained Sid. 'We booked our seats months ago, but we don't have to go…' He looked anxious.

'I took up the organ. I'm not very good, and it's just a hobby, but I belong to a group of enthusiasts, and once a year we invite a top professional organist to come along and do a recital. Some jazz things up a bit and offer a cabaret-type presentation.'

Sid's enthusiasm grew.

'They are all top-class performers and don't come cheap, I can tell you. We had to book tonight's personality a year in advance.'

Joy chimed in. 'We were going with some friends, but they're down with the flu, so we wondered if you two would like to come?'

'I'm up for it.' Ginger's reaction took me by surprise and pleased me no end. Music had played a huge part in my life until I had become unemployable, and the thought of a quality organist demonstrating his skills was most appealing.

'Count me in, for sure,' I responded enthusiastically.

Sid left the room temporarily, then returned brandishing a booklet. 'This is a programme for tonight's show; it tells you all you need to know.' He put it on a chair before leaving with Joy.

Ginger slid out of bed and picked up the programme. Back in bed, she began to read aloud. 'Brian Sharp' she said.

'What did you say?' The look of horror on my face told a story far better than words ever could.

'Something from your past?' Ginger looked agitated. 'You don't need to explain,' she added quickly, 'I'll get us out of it; leave it to me.'

'No…' I looked down at the duvet I had scrunched tight in reaction to the sound of my old friend's name, 'I'm done with running away.'

I began to explain my relationship with Brian Sharp.

'I first met Brian when I was booked to do a cabaret spot at an upmarket venue in Birmingham. It was prior to alcohol becoming the main man, although it was already big in my life.

'We hit it off straight away and after the show agreed to keep in touch, but as is often the case, it didn't happen. Then one morning, months later, the phone rang and it was Brian. He had undertaken a residency at the huge Stewart and Lloyds Steelworks Social Club, in Bilston Staffordshire, and had been let down by a singer/guitarist. He asked me if I could fill in.'

Ginger twisted in the bed to face me better.

'It was the first time I had played the social club, and the moment I walked in, I was struck by the size of the place. It was massive and already half full of people when I arrived for the band call at 6.30pm.

'Brian made a big fuss of me, and when my 45 minutes was on, the place was packed to the seams.'

I intended to give Ginger an abridged version of what happened.

'The evening went well. Brian and I complemented each other beautifully, and we even played an encore to the crowd. They went properly crazy for a Robert Earl number – '*I May Never Pass This Way Again*'. Truly off the scale. A week or so later, Brian rang me to ask if I would consider recording it with H&T Records in Birmingham, and I was thrilled by the idea.'

'That's amazing, Nick,' Ginger was clearly impressed.

'In the two years that followed, I frequently played with Brian, and the Robert Earl song always featured. Sadly, my drinking ruined me and took away my skills; Brian had no choice but to replace me. It all ended rather badly. I'm ashamed to say I threw up onstage, and then fell into the mess!' Ginger's face remained expressionless, and then she spoke softly.

'So, this will be a bittersweet reunion?'

'I'll try and keep out of his way,' I responded. 'I would hate to cast a shadow on your dad with the local organ fraternity. A drunken bum like me shouldn't besmirch your family's reputation.'

I settled back against the ornamentally carved headboard of the four-poster bed and immersed myself in the remembrances of my musical past. I closed my eyes, drifting on symphonic, euphonious imaginings, then spoke in tribute to a master of the modern musical art.

'All the singer's I have ever met who have been backed by Brian Sharp agree, it is like being transported to musical heaven on Celestial Sound. His capabilities are such, I would liken it to having a small orchestra behind you, it makes you supremely confident, you rise to greater heights, become invincible, indestructible... closer to God in fact.'

'He's that good, huh?'

'Oh yes, he's that good,' I replied.

*

Following a superb full English breakfast, Ginger decided she wanted to go to the nearest decent-size shopping centre. I guessed she wanted to look her best for her first public appearance in the village for five years, the family business was the main employer locally and it was understandable. I wondered what her mum and dad had used by way of an explanation for her sudden reappearance, and I thought it better if I knew, given the chances of such questions being asked of me in the hours to come.

Sid had offered the use of a car, and I was keen to accept; however, Ginger was determined to go by bus and I relented. We hadn't long to wait and neither did I for an answer to my question.

The bus was empty and the driver, a cheerful man probably in his fifties, accepted a travel permit of some sort and then gave her a second look.

'It can't be!' his voice was incredulous.

'Hello, Mr Gardener. Yes, it is me, and it's lovely to see you again.' He didn't seem to know what to say next, and with the sweetest of smiles she passed through into the seating area with me in her wake.

The bus made its way around the village, and soon we were on our way down country roads on the twenty-mile journey she had warned me of, and I decided there would never be a better time to ask.

'I'm bound to be asked about your missing years tonight, Ginger. What do you want me to say?'

'Just tell them to ask me.' Her reply came back so quickly it had to have been thought through, and probably discussed with her mum during their time together. Then she looked sideways at me and half-whispered, 'But you deserve to know the complexities.' She gazed into space and I knew how difficult the next moments were going to be.

'I knew nothing of it at the time, but my disappearance caused a major sensation. When I left, I drew out all my savings, but took nothing apart from what I stood up in. Following the abortion, heroin took me on a downward spiral and I was in a poor state when I somehow finished up on Dr Weiser's doorstep.'

'So that's how you met the Doc?' I interrupted in surprise.

Ginger nodded and then continued. 'He diagnosed a serious and total nervous breakdown, then found me a place in a psychiatric hospital. I was there for weeks, and then he was instrumental in me getting me my bedsit.

'Anyway, apart from being wealthy, Daddy is also very influential. Back here, when he and Mummy reported me missing, there was a great deal of local publicity and it even made the national papers. They had police officers staying in the house for weeks expecting a ransom demand, and all the time I was oblivious to it all. I was living in my own little cocoon of self-guilt because of what had happened to me, and the blame which I believed was mine. I came off the heroin while in hospital with the help of Buprenorphine, and later Methadone, and then stayed on that until I met you.

'Eventually, my case slipped down the police's pecking order, and Daddy employed a private detective which revealed nothing. Finally, they accepted I must be dead and went on to suffer more hell. Three years ago, an heiress's daughter – somewhere in the Midlands – was kidnapped and murdered, and my case surfaced once more. The perpetrator was questioned about me but, understandably, it came to nothing other than more suffering on Mummy and Daddy. How can I ever expect them to forgive me?'

For once, I was lost for words, and instead did the only thing I could do; I just held her hand.

'There is one thing I am committed to doing, and it has to be next week,' continued Ginger. 'I have to go with the family lawyer and make a statement at the police station so they can close the case. I am hoping you will come with me?' I nodded and spoke for the first time in a while. 'Of course I will; at least it will be closure for you all.'

I looked out of the window at the passing countryside.

'You got me thinking about my own situation,' I said. 'My family don't know whether I'm alive or dead. No one will care anyway; such is my badly scarred reputation!'

Now it was Ginger's turn to comfort me but I was past any form of condolence; my consolation was I had destiny to deal with. Ginger had the last word on the subject. 'So now you know why you have to point anyone making enquiries about my disappearance in my direction.'

*

Our shopping expedition turned out to be the best of medicine. Both of us withdrew into childlike behaviour, each of us trying on ridiculous fashion as well as smart and suitable clothes, and then Ginger broke the news that Sid had given her an envelope for me.

'Here it is, and there is a strange message to go with it, which he made me promise I wouldn't question you about. He said you would understand.'

'What is it?' I asked as she handed it to me, and she responded at once.

'He said… *If you are the wisest of men, you will accept this from the wisest of men.* Do you understand it, Nick?' This time it was my turn to answer immediately.

'Yes… absobloodylutely!' I replied.

I had been secretly concerned about what I was to wear at the Garden Theatre that night; no doubt it had crossed Ginger's mind too, and now the problem was solved thanks to Sid. Ginger purchased sensibly and looked sensational in both outfits she chose, and helped me when I confided it was a decade since I had bought anything new. New shoes were a novel experience, and so I felt both warmth and shame at the way I had allowed alcohol to all but destroy me and rob me of the self-respect I once held so dear. All too soon, we were on the bus and on our way back to 'Castle Keep'.

*

As the clock ticked towards 6pm, the time we planned to leave for the Garden Theatre, the atmosphere was tense and paradoxically frenetic. Ginger had discovered her father was now chairman of the organ society, and although he had an excellent team, much of the onus was on him. He was like the proverbial cat on a hot tin roof.

At last, it was time to depart, and Sid drove us the mile to the venue in the Jaguar, with Joy next to him and Ginger and me occupying the back seat. As soon as we arrived, Sid headed off to perform his duties, and I did my very best to act the perfect gentleman to both my ladies. Joy pointed to where the theatre bar was located (nervously out of consideration for me, I thought). I then dismissed the notion when she suggested I tried the local brew! Ginger looked at me and raised her eyes to the heavens, and I smiled and ordered lemonade for both of us and white wine for Joy.

'You don't have to make a sympathetic lemonade gesture, you know,' I whispered in her ear.

'I'm not. I never did like alcohol, and I made up my mind not to drink again several weeks ago.' I raised my eyebrows, too, and left it at that. I had just done so when I spotted Sid approaching us.

'Thank the heavens that's all done and dusted,' he remarked when he reached us, having shaken many hands on his return journey. 'Brian's a lovely man, and in the unanimous opinion of our membership, the top organist and showman in the country. It's taken us two years to get him here; that's how booked up he is. I'll introduce you to him later.' My blood ran cold! Ginger held my hand tightly.

Almost at once, a stream of local friends and acquaintances came up to say hello, although for the most part their interest was directed at Ginger. During the five-minute journey to the theatre, she had discretely asked me to call her Karrie, 'just for tonight', and I was pleased she had, as my intention was to use her birth name of Karen. I was quietly pleased with myself; I had been well brought up and etiquette was high on my parents' agenda. The fact it hadn't died a death in a gutter along the way was a relief; I knew only too well the importance of the propriety factor.

A voice over the intercom announced the fifteen-minute warning of the show's commencement, so glasses began to be emptied and people drifted towards the auditorium entrance. I smiled at the thought of not bothering to look to see if my glass was empty or not; there was nothing of value in it. Ginger smiled too;

I would never know, but I wondered if it was for the same reason.

'Mid-stalls, twelve rows from the front, just enough to get the feel and atmosphere of the audience, seats 44-47,' It was the first time I had seen and heard Sid in his element.

The lights lowered slowly and a deep male voice, with a breath of echo, announced, 'Ladies and Gentleman, it is with great pleasure, the Garden Theatre welcomes… Mr Brian Sharp!'

The members of the audience I had seen in the bar had struck me as a conservative lot, but the welcome that followed was deafening and took me completely by surprise. It was sensational, and without a doubt this was a man of legendary status revered in no uncertain terms.

The first half of the show ran over by ten minutes and yet seemed to go extremely quickly. I asked Ginger if it had done so for her, and she nodded then added she had been brought up on organ music and there were some of Brian's records in the family collection. I could see by her face that this was no ordeal, and I speculated on why she hadn't mentioned this when she had read from the programme Sid had left us.

Sid had reason to go backstage in the interval, and Ginger and I elected to stretch our legs. Joy said she was happy to stay put but might use the Ladies, and so we went our separate ways. Intervals were usually fifteen minutes, occasionally twenty, and so we had a quick breath of winter air and returned almost at once. As we negotiated the foyer, Ginger's voice grabbed my attention, 'Oh my God, No.' Sid was standing mid-floor, laughing and joking with none other than Brian Sharp.

'We've been looking for you two,' his voice rang out and the smiling pair walked towards us. It had been five years since we last met, but in a heartbeat he recognised me.

'Nick…! Nick Charles, what a surprise! How are you, and who is this lovely lady?' Brian's voice took over the moment, as his talent did on the stage. He was obviously pleased to see me again, and it enabled me to greet him similarly; we shook hands heartily, and then I remembered his question.

'Please meet Karrie, Sid Rigby-Jones' daughter. I'm staying with the family nearby.' Sid looked a little startled and was lost for words. At that moment, a three-minute warning of the show's commencement sounded and brought with it sense and reason.

'Stay behind afterwards, all of you. Whatever happens, don't shoot off without seeing me.' And Brian was gone.

I was glad Ginger spoke first; I wouldn't have known what to say.

'You know Nick has an alcohol problem, Daddy. Brian and Nick fell out over it a few years ago, although Brian doesn't seem to hold any grudges. We were frightened to tell you in case it spoilt your evening. We had no idea we would bump into him.' She expelled a lungful of air.

'You don't have to apologise, either of you. C'mon or we'll miss the show!'

The first twenty minutes following the interval were a selection of requests handed in by audience members, and then Brian Sharp at his organ-playing superlative best. He continued with thirty minutes of wartime classic movie theme tunes, and brilliantly edited wartime special battle effects from land, sea and air movie epics that simply blew the audience away. When during the *Dambusters March* pilots could be heard talking battle speak, the entire audience stood and gave an impromptu ovation. It was the highlight of the evening.

All good things come to an end, and when Brian finally left his organ and approached the microphone, I presumed it was to thank a very appreciative audience. Instead, I was in for a shock.

'Ladies and gentlemen,' he began. 'Several years ago, in one of the biggest clubs on the circuit, I received a request from a lady member of the audience for a song entitled, '*I May Never Pass This Way Again*'. A young man who was appearing on the show stepped forward to sing it, and such was the reaction we recorded it soon afterwards, and I am proud to say I arranged it. His name is Nick Charles, and he sits among you tonight. With your permission, I would like to end my show this evening with my arrangement and by asking him to join me on stage to sing it. Would you be so kind as to give a huge Garden Theatre welcome to… Nick Charles!'

Ginger told me later that the audience obliged with a rousing response. I have no recollection of this, only of the fear of the moment, knowing the only singing I had done for longer than I cared to remember was busking on Liverpool Street Station. I stood centre stage, spotlights bearing down relentlessly and then the Master struck up with the introduction. His skilled celestial sounds transported me to another place, another time.

How every note came out perfectly, I shall never know. Adrenalin, Brian's magic, fear of failure, God's will – perhaps all four – but it would remain a perplexing and enduring personal mystery.

When I rejoined the family, my shock reaction to proceedings had receded. I was now more in control and capable of handling the number of people milling around and enquiring about me. Fortunately, Brian appeared and rightly took over the clamouring numbers who all seemed to have a different question. I would have vied for their attention in my drinking days, now I did not, and it provided a sobering thought.

Abruptly, I realised Ginger was missing from the group, and I scanned the room, spotting her in conversation with a young man I estimated was around her own age. I had decided not to join them and was about to divert my attention when her eyes met mine. She appeared to take her leave and crossed the room to where I stood.

'An old school friend,' she mumbled, looking back in his direction only for me to observe he was looking in hers. Their visual connection lasted longer than was socially necessary, and I instinctively knew there was an emotional link. I was eight years older than Ginger, and if I gave thought to my own creed of drugs preventing mature growth, she could easily be still in her teens. Strangely, I did not feel any threat whatsoever. I only wanted the best for Ginger, and I loved her dearly, but I now knew I was not *in love* with her.

*

We continued to stay with Sid and Joy after the show, and two weeks later – when I recommenced my writing – I felt the call of the wild. I put my notes into a case I had bought with part of Sid's gift and set out to find Ginger. She was dressed for riding and was stroking Bruno's nose through the paddock rail. She turned as I approached, giving me a huge smile, but I was the first to speak.

'I think it's time to talk, Ginger.'

She nodded, 'I know, I had a long chat with Daddy a week ago, and he told me how honest you had been with him. They both love you very much, you know.' I looked at the ground and felt wretched. She took me by the hand and guided me from the paddock into the orchard, where the trees stood in neat rows.

'How do you think we should handle it, Nick?' Her hand was warm yet the tone matter of fact.

I looked at her realising how easy it would be to marry this lovely girl, but warning lights were flashing.

'I'm not being stubborn, but there are certain things I have to prove to myself. I'm *one drink* away from skid row, and you know that. At the same time, I know that my life and the lives of hundreds I have met and recorded must stand as a testimony of alcohol awareness. I need to focus on my work. And that means returning to the Doc.'

Ginger looked at me thoughtfully and then said, 'I think I knew all along; I just wanted to enjoy it while I could. To me, you were the first taste of kindness and caring I had experienced since the assault that changed my life.'

We were still holding hands when we re-entered the paddock, and she added, 'I won't ever be going back to London, Nick. I feel I would rather stay here with Mummy and Daddy and hopefully make up for some of the heartache I have caused… In any case, I belong here.'

I nodded in agreement, but with a deep sadness and a terrible feeling that I was making a huge mistake. Yet, I was aware of the logic in what both she and I had said.

'How shall we explain?' I managed.

Ginger considered things, momentarily, and then said in a whisper, 'Leave it to me, Nick,' I can do that after you've gone.

*

Sid was out quoting on a job, and Joy at the hairdressers in the town where Ginger and I had done our shopping. We ate lunch in relative silence and then set off to the railway station. I have no way of describing how I felt as we made our way down the driveway from the house and turned towards the village. Ten times, at least, I nearly stopped and said to hell with destiny; I was acutely aware how all of this could so easily have been a part of me, and me a part of it.

We stood alone as the branch line diesel slowed to a stop, the impersonal atmosphere cloaking the sadness we both felt. I hugged Ginger and we held each other tightly. I tried to picture the late scene where the catering caravan stood that served people of the night, those with nowhere to go, and where she and I had first met. I could not.

I let myself into a compartment and pulled down the window. Within seconds, the guard blew his whistle and the train began to pull out of the station. 'You will write, won't you, Nick?'

'Of course, Ginger. Of course I will.'

We blew kisses and waved, yelling above the noise.

'See you soon! Take care, I love you...!'

'God bless you, Karen Rigby-Jones,' was my final dispatch, and I am sure the blood drained from her face as she realised the words signalled her return to normality and my final goodbye and return to...! I knew not what.

I watched her red hair disappear into the distance… I didn't write, and neither could she without a return address.

I never saw Ginger again.

Real Time - my final brush with skid row, 1976. I am bottom-left, with the umbrella. Reproduced with the kind permission of Marketa Luskacova.

Salvation Army Hostel 1974/5 (photo taken in 1977, my last SA bed, to the left of middle pillar).

This was the attic at the Spitalfields School building which had room for two beds. This was mine I used in 1974/5, still in situ when this picture was taken in 1977. The door had been secured and we obtained permission from the demolition Works Manager to break down the door.

SA Canteen - I am sat behind the pillar with two old dosser friends who were still there. This was taken in 1977. Sentimental journey.

Mobile Café Spitalfields, where I met Ginger in 1976, still in place here in 1978.

I woke here on my last day on the streets, December 13th, 1976, 6am. I staggered to an early opener for a bottle, changed my mind, then went to the public baths instead. Then, I headed to the Marquis of Granby, Dean Bradley Street, Westminster, at 11.30am, and drank half a pint of bitter - my last ever drink. A job as a detoxing barman beckoned at the nearby Barley Mow.

This was a place of great foreboding.
While parts of it were still used, it often offered a place to doss.
My outstanding recollection was unidentifiable sounds
(probably creaking).

This was a hostel for homeless and destitute women of all ages.
In exchange for a drink, they would do sewing, darning, and
often exchange clothing vouchers for second-hand clothes
stores, which they seemed to magic from nowhere.

I spent many a night in custody here, being allowed to sleep in a chair while sobering up. This day was a journey of remembrance.

My first holiday following my recovery.
I was completely overwhelmed.

My first house with Kelly, Hounslow, 1983.
New two-tone Ford Capri.

My Investiture at Buckingham Palace in 1997 with Prince Charles. We discussed the alcohol problem.

The Chaucer Clinic Team. (Left to Right) Nikki de Villiers, Nick Charles, Lesley Charles, Teresa Weiler.

13: TURNING POINT

There were thirty minutes between departing the branch line train and catching my London connection, and I spent them well, selecting a flask-shaped, half-sized bottle of expensive brandy.

I was pleased when I eventually joined the London train, contented by the fact there were few stops and few passengers.

Once on the train, I broke the seal with a profound reverence, took an innocuous paper cup from my business case, and poured some brandy to the halfway mark with great care. Thirty seconds later, the Rigby-Jones family were history.

As the train clattered along and the alcohol played its deadly game, any thoughts of regret or notions of a second point of no return disappeared into the delusionary alcohol ether. What useful purpose would it serve if I was right and, like Jim Conway, I finished up in a bed with metal sides wearing a nappy? I already knew full well and indeed advocated that there was a second and final point of no return; I had seen the proof often enough. I had been alcohol-free for almost six months, and my present task was to see if I could abstain for the weeks to come once I had emptied this bottle. I was mindful it would not be the first time I had put myself to the test, vowing it would be my final experiment. The truth was, I wanted to drink. Had I already passed the final point of no return? I simply wanted to prove I was not powerless over alcohol. The fact I was in my fourteenth year of trying had apparently taught me nothing.

*

I regained consciousness in the old Spitalfields School's Assembly Hall, once pointed out to me almost affectionately the first night I met Ginger. It had served for generations of morning prayers, school plays, and lessons of many descriptions, but now lay in desecrated ignominy. The drapes were still in place as were the stage curtains, and the odd chair too. Sadly, there was crushed plaster and masonry covering the floor;

broken bricks, too, and with little evidence of where they had come from. The excrement up the walls was more easily explained. I counted fourteen comatose shapes of lowlife within these once proud, even hallowed walls, and no doubt some of the unwanted filth had belonged to them.

The foul smell which accompanied the depravity began to register in my nostrils and take its place alongside the squalor, and I wondered how such degeneracy could exist in modern society. I looked at the unconscious, once human shapes and thought out loud.

'What a useless pile of shit!'

The abruptness of my words in the silence inspired movement amongst some of the corpses in waiting, and one of them – a yard along to the right of where I lay – spoke back.

'Do you mean the stuff on the walls, or us lying here… including you?'

I looked down at the clothes that had so recently hung in an expensive wardrobe and tried to work out how long ago it had been since an heiress wanted to marry me. Several days at least, I decided, and then I remembered the money. In a frantic movement, my hand shot towards my inside jacket pocket, but a dreadful pain stopped the movement and made me bite my lip, and it was my other arm that told me there was nothing left of Sid's gift.

'Fuck you,' I said with venom to the bedmate on my right, who so recently had been Karen Rigby-Jones.

A flash of memory reminded me I had bought some foam insoles for my new shoes, and had put an equal wad of twenty-pound notes between them and the leather in each. I reached painfully to remove one of them, but my feet wore only socks! The renegades had benefited from more than just my money!

I recalled a whole section I had written about how alcohol affects all aspects of the nervous system, and was glad they lay safe and warm in carrier bags at the Doc's surgery. I desperately tried to put into place the events since leaving 'Castle Keep'. I was okay up until opening the bottle on the train, and then things got vague. I had shadowy recollections of getting off the train in London and catching a tube, then standing in a bar flashing my cash – a fatal flaw in the deluded mind of a drunk. And then there was a fight! This prompted the recall of the pain in my arm, now made worse as a result of reaching hurriedly to retrieve money that wasn't there. I tried to move and screamed out in pain. There were several scuffles that came from different directions as animal-like shapes disappeared through a doorway that had no door. I had to get to a hospital even though the Doc was an easily accessible distance away. I couldn't face him yet, even though I was still fortified; I might have a greater need for him later. The withdrawal was yet to come!

A worn-out pair of boots caught my eye, and I knew how they got there. I struggled into them with difficulty and stumbled out through the doorway, although more slowly than the other corpses had done. The mile and a half to St Leonard's hospital took an age, and on arrival I was crying in pain. I was taken to a side room; a doctor came and gave me an injection, and I woke up in bed on a ward.

'I don't know any details, I'm afraid, but I think it was a dislocation of sorts, but the doctor will explain in the morning.' The nurse replying to my question was oriental, very pretty and smiled reassuringly. The arm was bandaged and sore but no longer so painful, and I was able to move it a little and promptly went to sleep. It was in the early hours when I woke again and picked up on my meanderings about alcohol and the nervous system. I thought over how it manifested itself, and for a while I couldn't get the dead brain of Jim Conway out of my head, and his words Mama, Dada, Vera and Nick.

In practical terms, I believed the first sign of alcohol creating damage to the nervous system was difficulty remembering what happened during the previous night's boozy session. I was also a believer in the theory that blackouts occurred long before anyone realised their connection to alcohol. How could they know? Even in the modern day, there are precious few influential and logically explained advanced notices of alcohol's vicious capabilities. Most alcohol messages are bright, sparkling, advertising presentations, with beautiful people extolling the wonders of partying on one sensational boozy product or another. Their main purpose is to impress how wonderful life is with a glass in your hand.

Abruptly I remembered my work currently lay unfinished with the Doc. It had to be completed satisfactorily, or my life experiences would have all been for nothing, and there was so much that people needed to know. After that, it was down to individuals whether to drink or not.

I was only too aware that few people knew the difference between blacking out and passing out. Many were surprised when I explained that passing out is to be unconscious, but blacking out is to appear fairly normal outwardly, but upon returning from the episode, have no recollection of the blackout period. The length of blackouts varies dramatically from a few minutes upwards. I had once suffered the terrifying ordeal of coming to, on the seafront of a northern seaside town, with absolutely no recollection of how I came to be there or, in fact, of the previous three days. There was no straightforward *'cannot remember the night before'* element to this experience, and I could testify to a further disturbing and extremely frightening blackout period that occurred a year or so later.

It happened in springtime, and my first conscious awareness that it had taken place was the sun shining and a terrible headache. In physical terms, it was like regaining consciousness in the very act of doing or saying something, in this case taking part in a conversation without knowing what it was about.

I found myself sat on a bench, situated on the corner of an avenue and a main road, two hundred yards from where I lived with my wife and daughter.

Usually, I had a bottle of cider when sat in this particular place, but today I didn't… and there was something else odd, too. I felt damp and unusually cold. I looked at my watch to see how late I was for lunch… or was it dinner? The timepiece was missing; had I been out all night? I now realised the importance of putting together recent events, but I couldn't remember a thing; no continuity, no recent memories at all!

I began to realise something was seriously wrong; there was a huge gap in my memory. Suddenly I became aware of a man sitting next to me offering a bottle of cider. Swigging from the bottle gave me the courage to ask how long I had been there. He cackled and then spoke in a phlegmy voice, *'You're having one of them, aren't you?'* I paused, then nodded. We'd both been there before.

Then hysteria gripped me. I thought of my wife and daughter and struggled yet again to remember how long I'd been away. I broke into a run towards home, which was a tatty farmhouse turned into flats. It wasn't far, but after twenty or thirty yards, I fell exhausted onto the pavement. I was fighting for breath and in pain everywhere. I struggled to my feet and, with a superhuman effort, broke into a jog and swung left into the drive where my flat was… or rather where it should have been! The momentum of my effort sent me crashing over a low wall into a neat garden. Cut and bruised, I staggered to my feet and looked towards where the farmhouse flats should have been. Instead… there stood two bungalows in pretty gardens!

Behind me, a female voice spoke my name, asking if she could help and I struggled to see through a mass of tears. It was a neighbour, and she mentioned a cup of tea. Soon, I was struggling to drink it, both hands shaking violently, liquid splashing everywhere.

'Where's my flat? Where's my home gone?' I managed. 'Where are my wife and baby?'

She looked at me sadly, and held my hand.

'You left here when your wife divorced you. They knocked the flats down and built bungalows six years ago. We objected to the plans at first, but… I'm so sorry, Nick, you must let me get you some help… you see… your wife has remarried and has new babies.'

An ambulance arrived. Accident and Emergency was my first port of call before I was admitted to a psychiatric establishment where I lost more of my memory, but this time to seriously heavy medication.

Eventually, my body and mind returned to a semblance of order. I was told I had suffered a severe alcohol-induced blackout and was lucky there appeared to be no lasting damage.[1]

*

'Can't you sleep?' The voice brought me back to the present and belonged to the pretty oriental nurse, and I shook my head.

'Would you like a cup of tea?' she asked, and I nodded. She walked away but soon returned and put a large mug on my locker and a finger to her lips, indicating the international signal of silence.

I lay in a half-light, illuminated by a distant fully-lit corridor and a single bulb beneath the nursing station, and drifted back to long-gone days.

There was no set or chronological order of things as my usually active mind spent the time looking back over my life. First of all, I found myself back in my childhood and – as I was growing up – being bullied both physically and psychologically (although more often the latter).

As I mused, I suddenly switched and found myself on stage at a major venue in a glittering suit, or confusingly lying drunk – in squalor – on the floor of a disused building that was set for demolition. In brief waking moments, I pondered which would come first, a total nervous breakdown from which I would never successfully recover, or multiple organ failure.

As the minutes ticked away, I deliberated upon when I had definitively crossed the indefinable line from social drinker to fully-blown addict. Abruptly, the flashing images of my mother's discriminatory views, which caused me such distress, presented an indication of when this had come about. Her racial views were not just reserved to colour, and when I brought a pretty Irish girl for tea one Sunday, I was threatened with a fate worse than death if I were to repeat the performance. However, this time I rebelled and left home, despite the fact it meant camping out at my girlfriend's parents' home for a few weeks.

During this stay, I was gifted a bottle of Poteen 90% ABV (a traditional Irish beverage) and drank the lot in a few hours of isolation while everyone was at work. As a consequence, I suffered what I now know was an alcohol seizure. From that moment onwards, alcohol's effect upon me changed forever, and any resistance I may have had disappeared – leaving behind a craving that occurred on a daily basis.

Within six months, I was unemployable and my personality irreparably damaged. Interestingly, in later years when I began counselling, one of my leading questions was, 'Did you have a defining moment when you crossed the invisible line into alcoholism?' Those who conceded they had numbered around 50%.

Back in my bed, it was my childhood again. I was six, maybe seven, and kneeling at my bedside, saying my prayers before sleep.

'Please, Jesus, help me *not* to be sad tomorrow.'

Abruptly, everything flooded back. The torment of what I now recognised as acute anxiety; something I had suffered on an ongoing basis since my early childhood.

In those far-off days, the rural county police force was an extended family, and I had aunties and uncles in profusion. This may have been born out of the fact that the war had created a special bond of heroes, and a camaraderie that was unshakable. This was a generation who had pulled together in a manner beyond the comprehension of many. In that moment, I realised the greatest influence in my life was having been educated by men and women who had just won the Second World War. They had done so with discipline, tenacity, wisdom, perceptibility, enthusiasm, inspiration, and courage. All these elements would reach out to me when I needed them most, and save my life.

I was still left with sadness and anxiety, except the WWII spirit of people helping people was about to bring help my way big time. One day, my mother overheard me saying my prayers and sat me down and confided she was often sad and anxious too. She said there was nothing anyone could do, so we had to get a grip and fight it; go for a brisk walk or a run, ride your bike like the wind, or sing your favourite hymn or song loudly. I felt better just listening to her words, and sometimes her advice worked. But not always so, and I told her.

One day we had a visit from my uncle James who I loved dearly. He had a stern exterior, and then turned into a teddy bear when he thought no one was looking. He asked me about my sadness and told me he was a man of medicine, a kind of doctor, and he wanted to help me with the way I often felt. He asked lots of questions and then returned several days later with a box of tiny yellow tablets, and we had a secret chat. He said I was to tell Mum when I was sad and she would let me have one, but I must never take more than one in any one day, and I was to try not to take them regularly. I kept my word and eventually forgot I had them because the sadness and anxiety had gone away.

In my teens, the symptoms returned, and one day – when I was particularly low – Dad took me to the pub to cheer me up and bought me my first alcoholic drink. A half-pint of beer had the same effect as one of the little yellow tablets, and I felt saved; for a while, I was happy… too happy. When I drank too much, the sadness was a hundred times worse in the aftermath, but a quick drink soon put it right… although not for long. Instead, I entered into a spiral of self-destruction that destroyed everything I held dear and nearly killed me.

I was admitted to hospital on several occasions for the process called detoxification, which got me better so I could drink alcohol again, but I was soon back to square one. During one such stay, I confided in a friendly charge nurse and told him of my long-dead uncle James and his tiny magic yellow tablets, and he promised to make some enquiries. A day or so later, he arrived with a friendly consultant who asked searching questions and made lots of notes; they both went away but my charge nurse friend returned later. He said I was to let him know when I felt sad again and a day or so later, when the awful symptoms returned, I let him know at once.

He produced a box of tablets which were small but not yellow and my heart sank. 'Try one,' was all he said, and unforgettably the effect was the same as with my long-gone wonderful tiny yellow ones. 'What are they?' I enquired, determined not to lose track of them ever again.

'Dextropropoxyphene,' he replied. 'But there's a problem. They may be banned because a large number of people who are using them are committing suicide. I'm afraid the medication is getting the blame.'

Nevertheless, they worked for me, and I was able to secure a supply for some considerable time, but the ban was eventually implemented, and soon after, my personal hell returned. There was always some other routine anxiety medication available, but they did little other than turn me into a zombie. Anyway, there was always alcohol, of course! Sadly, all it succeeded in doing was to introduce me to total destitution and I became an outcast; all I had left to comfort me was the drink!

It would be four long years before I remembered the words of the caring Sergeant Campbell, and realised it wasn't that alcohol was one of many problems in my life, but that my problem in life *was* alcohol!

---

[1] I picked up other information, too. Alcohol excess first affects the part of the brain that rationalises behaviour and control. The correct functioning of these controls gets impaired as soon as *any* alcohol reaches the brain, causing a person to be less inhibited or more confident. What is actually happening is the ability to make carefully thought-out decisions is being hindered. The hospital psychiatrist told me alcohol affects the brain for long periods. As an example, one pint of beer for about three hours, two pints of beer for about six hours, and three pints of beer for about nine hours. Some effects still remain after the alcohol has left the brain and body; a good example being the hangover. In my case, the outcome was catastrophic!

In addition, he added, around seventy per cent of all alcohol abusers show brain damage on scans, and excessive drinking can act on the deeper centres of the brain causing coma and death.

Blackouts or complete memory lapses are common and headaches can be very frequent. Alcohol seizures can be caused by a high alcohol intake, usually in withdrawal which is shakes, known as delirium tremens, dry mouth, sweating, palpitations, panic attacks, anxiety and acute fear. Head injuries, sometimes resulting in brain damage are common amongst alcohol abusers.

14: A STEP UP THE LADDER

Discharge came more quickly than I would have liked. My arm remained painful and I felt far from well, although I had no idea why. If it was alcohol withdrawal, it was a different version to the one I was used to. The hospital doctor explained he thought the arm may have been dislocated in the assault and had gone back into place, either by itself or during the fracas. He mentioned the possibility I could have sustained ligament damage which, as a result, could take time to heal completely, and to be aware of the fact. His final act was charitable and more than I deserved. My oriental nurse pushed me in a wheelchair to a second-hand clothing store nearby and decked me out in a new wardrobe, including an overcoat. After she had paid, she informed me the doctor had given her the money out of his own pocket. I felt extremely grateful and inordinate shame in equal measures.

I made my way to the hostel and was greeted by a familiar face on the reception. He enquired how the detox had gone, and it took a while to sink in that it was Ginger's to which he referred. Time was not a measurement in this world, only an inevitability. I asked to speak to someone senior, and they came quickly, and I handed over a hospital letter requesting I be allowed to stay in during the day for two weeks. It was granted. It also recommended I go out for exercise and fresh air for short spells; I felt like I had won a prize.

For the most part, I slept a lot and spent a great deal of time researching alcohol consumption and dependency in Bishopsgate Library, and making notes on paper kindly donated by the young woman who worked there. I sketched out two graphs and asked if it was possible for her to do the layout for me and she did so, and even returned them to me in a card folder. There had been a time when I could tell from the way she looked at me that she thought I was an undesirable, probably a waste of space. Perhaps it was the heavy bandage on my arm which changed her mind, or then again it may have been that I was clean and tidy!

I was never quite sure what day it was, and asked her often. One morning, I bought a single rose for her with my Scarborough Street handout, then hadn't the courage to give it to her, so I left it on the counter when she wasn't looking. Later, I noticed it had been put into a small glass vase and placed next to where she sat on the occasions I interrupted her with tiresome queries and requests. She will never know, but just seeing her – neat, tidy, clean, and normal – provided me with the hope and inspiration I so desperately needed in the weeks that followed. I stayed in at the hostel during the day for a month, maybe more, before anyone realised I had overstayed, and even then I was only prompted gently. I needed a shove, and it did me good; it was time to pick up the pieces and the moment had arrived.

*

It was a desperately cold morning when I decided to visit Dr Weiser and confess my drunken shame. I knew he would welcome me as a long-lost friend, and the guilt I felt for not keeping in touch with him was huge. Following his customary hug, I struggled to find the words of contrition I owed him and which he so richly deserved, but he stopped me. Instead, he offered a message in his unforgettable accent.

'There is a film called, *The Day the Earth Stood Still*.' In it, an alien force made everything on the planet come to a temporary halt, and I want you to imagine this has happened to you. All you have to do is re-emerge from the moment you arrived here today, as though nothing has happened since the instant you departed. There will be no inquest, no blame, no recriminations, and no conscience to answer to. Look forward not back. For you, the earth is now moving once more.' I was grateful the Doc never mentioned Ginger.

Silence dominated, and then I spoke because I knew he wanted me to.

'I've… got my lecture ready for Saturday night, Doc. Would you like me to put the posters up?'

'Yes, of course, my boy,' he responded at once. 'But, first, we go to the café, for breakfast.' I vowed never to forget the joy that forgiveness brings.

Eating together seemed like old times. On our return to the surgery, I asked politely for my carrier bags and sat in Ginger's old seat in front of the typewriter she had made her own. I was amazed how far she had progressed, and I tapped out with two fingers from where she had left off to the background of the Doc busying himself. It was an hour before either of us spoke, and I was relieved I didn't have to try and sound normal by being first.

'You're getting faster! Had you realised?' I looked at him, puzzled for several seconds, and then the penny dropped. 'I don't think I'll make a typing pool somehow, but I do seem to have gained some confidence,' I replied and then gritted my teeth hard in a token of strength I didn't feel – to stop thinking of how much I missed Ginger.

'I've got to take a prescription to the hostel. Will you be okay on your own for half an hour or so, Nick?' I nodded and he concluded, 'We'll go for lunch as soon as I get back,' and he was gone before I could reply.

I had been wondering about employment but the options were limited as I had no qualifications. Driving of some sort was an option, except I had no idea what had happened to my driving licence. On impulse, I decided to write to my father and ask if there was any way he would, or could, help me. I struggled with the words but told the truth exactly as it was, and crossed the road to a post box that was directly opposite. I had typed at least two further pages before the Doc returned and we adjourned for lunch.

I received a friendly welcome home from the staff at the Doc's favourite lunchtime eating place, and as soon as the waiter disappeared with our order, Dr Weiser leaned forward to speak with a concentrated expression.

'I have been asked to do a series of talks at rather contrasting venues on the subject of alcohol addiction and the ramifications. I would like you to accompany me in a supporting role and make presentations like you do at your Saturday night lectures. Would you be so kind as to oblige me…? We will get paid, of course,' he added, almost as an afterthought.

I was stunned, and looked at him vacantly until I realised my mouth was open. I pulled myself together, remembering how much I owed this man, and I was not about to refuse him, despite great trepidation.

'There will be six altogether, each of an hour's duration, with a thirty-minute question and answer session afterwards,' he continued. 'We will have plenty of time to plan and rehearse, of course, and they are all in London.' Suddenly, I burst out laughing but stopped abruptly when I realised he looked hurt.

'I'm sorry, Doc. I wasn't laughing at you. It's just the absurdity of someone suddenly discovering your value and maybe of mine too. Of course, I will accompany you!'

The Doc smiled.

'I showed a doctor friend your words,' he explained, 'and he asked my permission to reproduce some of them. He even quoted your opening line to me – 'Alcohol is a perpetrator of more deaths, physical and psychological damage, health conditions, and human misery than will ever be known. Then, a few days later, I received a letter asking me to attend a District Health Authority meeting, where I was asked by the Chief Executive if I would consider taking on a number of lectures for the benefit of health professionals.'

Lunch arrived and the theme of our conversation was distracted by more mundane matters. Over coffee, though, the thread of our projected talks resumed.

'I have found alcohol addiction to be a condition which would be better called, *I ain't got it*,' I said. 'I'll open the first talk with that. The vast majority of drinkers, and this which will include our audience, will always strongly deny there is anything wrong with their drinking; we are going to have a fight on our hands.'

'It is true,' said the Doc. 'Denial is everywhere.'

'It would be helpful if we offered some sort of tool which can indicate who is dependent and who isn't,' I volunteered cheerfully. 'And we *must* introduce a more constructive detoxification programme. After twenty-odd detoxes, I can tell you the only absolutely safe and comfortable one I have ever endured was when you allowed me extra medication.'

I sat back in my chair and used my serviette as a gesture of completion, rather more than for conventional use, and waited for his response.

'This is good, Nick,' he said firmly and looked pleased. 'Can you put together these tools in time? The first talk is in a month.'

'Well, funny you should ask. I've just completed first drafts on both,' I replied. 'I call the first one the ACR, the Alcohol Consumption Regime!'

*

For some unaccountable reason, it was always the Doc's habit to make a pot of tea as soon as we returned from lunch, and this day would be no exception. I took advantage of him being distracted to retrieve the safely stored sheets of paper my librarian lady had placed in a firm office folder, and put them in a space I cleared on his desk. He soon arrived with two steaming mugs of tea, and looked down at the neat A4 presentations with keen interest. 'It's only brief, and I will explain it,' I said hurriedly, as he placed two pages side by side. 'As you can see, the first is a two-week regime split into three eight-hour sessions: sleeping time, working time, and social time.' He studied it intently.

Week 1

TIME	MIDNIGHT TO 8 AM	8 AM TO 4 PM	4 PM TO MIDNIGHT
MONDAY	NO DRINKING ALLOWED	NO DRINKING ALLOWED	NO DRINKING ALLOWED
TUESDAY	NO DRINKING ALLOWED	DRINKING ALLOWED	NO DRINKING ALLOWED
WEDNESDAY	NO DRINKING ALLOWED	NO DRINKING ALLOWED	DRINKING ALLOWED
THURSDAY	DRINKING ALLOWED	NO DRINKING ALLOWED	DRINKING ALLOWED
FRIDAY	DRINKING ALLOWED	DRINKING ALLOWED	DRINKING ALLOWED
SATURDAY	NO DRINKING ALLOWED	NO DRINKING ALLOWED	DRINKING ALLOWED
SUNDAY	NO DRINKING ALLOWED	DRINKING ALLOWED	NO DRINKING ALLOWED

Week 2

TIME	MIDNIGHT TO 8 AM	8 AM TO 4 PM	4 PM TO MIDNIGHT
MONDAY	DRINKING ALLOWED	DRINKING ALLOWED	NO DRINKING ALLOWED
TUESDAY	NO DRINKING ALLOWED	DRINKING ALLOWED	DRINKING ALLOWED
WEDNESDAY	DRINKING ALLOWED	DRINKING ALLOWED	DRINKING ALLOWED
THURSDAY	NO DRINKING ALLOWED	NO DRINKING ALLOWED	NO DRINKING ALLOWED
FRIDAY	DRINKING ALLOWED	NO DRINKING ALLOWED	NO DRINKING ALLOWED
SATURDAY	NO DRINKING ALLOWED	DRINKING ALLOWED	NO DRINKING ALLOWED
SUNDAY	DRINKING ALLOWED	DRINKING ALLOWED	DRINKING ALLOWED

My explanation tumbled out, 'It's a serious test of an individual's alcohol dependence. A lot of people will find it difficult, and will fall at the first fence – that is in the first 24 hours; most regular drinkers will struggle. Those who are worryingly dependent, either cannot or will not attempt it. The most troubled of all will rubbish it, and consider the test beneath them. There will be a number who will fail in secret.'

'Well…!' was his single, first-word reaction, as he sat up straight in his chair. I stared and waited. 'I think it's a *first,* Nick. I agree we should use it.'

I breathed a sigh of relief and then reached for the single sheet which remained in the folder and held it close to my chest.

'The second important point was a safe and efficient detox programme.'

'Yes, of course.' His expression was of deep concentration.

'The librarian typed this out too,' I added.

Unexpectedly, his eyes lit up and a broad smile appeared on his face.

COMMUNITY DETOXIFICATION REGIME USING CHLORDIAZEPOXIDE (LIBRIUM) 1975

TIME	Day 1	Day 2	Day 3	Day 4	Day 5	Day 6	Day 7	Day 8
9.00 am	30 mg	25 mg	20 mg	15 mg	10 mg	5 mg	5 mg	
1.00 pm	30 mg	25 mg	20 mg	15 mg	10 mg	5 mg		
5.00 pm	30 mg	25 mg	20 mg	15 mg	10 mg	5 mg		
10.00 pm	30 mg	25 mg	20 mg	15 mg	10 mg	5 mg	5 mg	5 mg

He continued to examine the document, but there was more I wanted to say and so I interrupted his thoughts.

'I don't mean any disrespect Doc, but your detox method – which works very well, I hasten to add – is based on how us dossers are when we present to you each day at your surgery. You couldn't possibly give us any more medication because it would probably finish up being sold illegally, so yours is the only way it can be done.'

I shuffled a little on my feet. 'But, in the real world, people live in houses with others who love and care for them; theirs is a whole different ball game, and it's the community at large that our talks are going to be scrutinised for. That said, I am convinced the illustrated doses are not high enough to entirely eradicate alcohol seizures or fits, as we call them on the streets. My ideal format would be to extend the detox to 10 days, starting with a higher dose.'

Dr Weiser scratched his head and looked puzzled, and instead of making a comment, he waited for me to continue. I took a deep breath.

'This series of lectures has been instigated because of *your* experiences and all you have told them about me. Please don't be offended, but people are not even remotely interested in those like me on the streets; unlike you they couldn't care less whether we live or die. They're becoming aware of the effect alcohol is having on the health service, industry, crime and maybe even underage drinking, and they want to know if we have a silver bullet. Perhaps we do, but only if we do it our way.' I sat down and waited for his reaction.

He stuck a thumbnail between two teeth and screwed his face up in a manner of deep thought, and I waited.

He looked back down at my librarian's graph and then turned to face me.

'What are you saying precisely, Nick? I don't want to waste time playing cat and mouse with them?'

'I am saying we should plan a quality lecture that covers the *general public* and its drinking habits, not those we work with on the streets. Let's blow the medics away with the facts and our know-how. We have no need to worry, Doc... the streets will still be here when we get back!'

'Okay, then that is what we will do.' The Doc surprised me with the rapidity of his decision, and on this occasion, there was no time to ponder.

*

My first ever detox was in Birmingham and it was so amateur it was pathetic. There were a dozen of us in a ward, and after the first day, we were only given medication when we asked for it. Four patients had alcohol withdrawal seizures, and in addition to them, I'm pretty sure I had one too. But mine occurred at night and I mainly slept through it. It was a total shambles, and I was the only one who lasted the week's duration.

One good thing did come out of my stay, however. I heard about detox units being run in both convents and monasteries in the Shires and was given a few addresses. I arrived at one of these in a poor state. I convinced the receiving monk that I knew all about alcohol detoxification and – naively – he agreed for me to set my own medication reduction scale. Without labouring the story, when my detox was completed I offered to stay on and assist the brothers with other patients, and do odd jobs to earn my keep. I stayed six months using the reduction plan, and they were impressed because I cut the alcohol seizure or fit rate from 25% to 10%.

One of the monks confided in me that, at one time, they were having so many seizures the Abbot was considering withdrawing the service. I was pleased in one way, but remained unhappy about the 10%. It was at that time I recognised the strength of alcohol the drug, and figured that if we raised the detox medication to a sensible level, we would achieve a nil seizure rate.

*

Back in the Doc's office, there was one of the familiar silences I had come to expect when the Doc was meditating. So, I sat and waited, scribbling a few notes that came to mind as I did so. Then he came to life but not with what I expected.

'Do you think you may have had your last drink, Nick?'

I gripped the pen in my hand tightly and couldn't look him in the eyes, and so replied whilst looking at the floor.

'I'm not going to lie to you, Doc. The answer is no, but I *am* sure it's not far away. In fact, I feel it is closer than ever before, but you have my word it will not interfere with our lecture presentations.' He nodded, but there was a look of sadness in his eyes which I couldn't help noticing.

Then, he seemed to take heart, and with fresh zest passed me a sheet of paper. 'Here are the lecture dates, venues, times.'

I looked at the dates on the sheet. The first one was just a month away, 'Plenty of time to get it all together,' I commented.

'Agreed,' he said. 'We begin now!'

15: A VISIT FROM THE PAST

I was met back at the hostel by the beaming face of my favourite desk clerk, who seemed even keener to welcome me than usual.

'You never told me you used to be a superstar!' He may have had a big smile on his face, but he sounded indignant. I looked at him puzzled, and my expression must have suggested further information would be appreciated.

'Roger Lavern out of the *Tornados* has been here looking for you!'

I was aghast, ashamed, or maybe both that Roger had discovered where I lived, and stood waiting for further information.

'They were my favourite instrumental group. The first British instrumental group to make number one in America!' The clerk stood looking at me with what, I think, may have been admiration and then added, 'He said you used to be his singer; anyway, he's coming back later.' I winced and turned towards the concrete staircase, but his voice sounded again. 'There's a letter here for you, Nick.'

It was postmarked my home village, and I opened it at once, wondering who it could be from. Out fell my driving licence, a single pound note, and a short letter from my father.

> Dear Nick,
>
> Thank you for your letter, as you will see I have managed to persuade the authorities to renew your driving licence as it had only recently expired, and I do hope it helps you find employment.
>
> We thought you were probably dead, and so it has given us fresh hope you will find your way in the world and perhaps one day we will be able to talk proudly of you again.
>
> Your mother is quite frail and her mind is not as well as it once was, the doctor thinks it may be down to worry.
>
> I have enclosed £1, I haven't sent more because I know it will only go across some bar or another, I would be pleased if you would spend it on some decent food.

Roger Lavern came to see us recently looking for you, and I gave him your address, I hope you don't mind.

Dad

I turned away from the desk clerk so he couldn't see the tears on my cheeks and took to the stairs even though we were supposed to stay in the common room until after 8pm. He didn't challenge me, and I guessed he must have witnessed my distress. I lay on my bed and was deep in thought when the same clerk came to tell me Roger Lavern had arrived.

There he was in reception, larger than life. To a growing audience, he was describing being on tour with international superstars and signing autographs. Surrounded by others, who were homeless like me, I wasn't sure if his graciousness said much about him… or something about me!

Roger and I walked down Bishopsgate to a restaurant where I had washed up in the kitchens on numerous occasions. He bought me a coffee.

'What is it you want?' I asked without feeling.

'I can help you, if you want me to,' he responded.

'Help me to do what exactly, Roger?' I realised there was no good reason to take my plight out on him, and apologised at once. 'Sorry, mate, this is my mess, not yours.' There was a pause while a waiter delivered our coffees; he waited to respond.

'I'm doing private cabaret bookings, mainly at stately piles. The Tornados fame stuck, and my piano playing is in demand, especially since I came back from Mexico. Did you read about me in the nationals?'

'Sorry. I'm a bit out of touch with the mainstream.' He looked at me and for the first time since his arrival, I think realisation dawned.

'Do you want to talk about it?'

'No,' I answered immediately.

After half an hour of one-sided chat, I think he grasped I was making little contribution to the proceedings, and this was not the Nick he knew. It was therefore – with unexpected enthusiasm – that he turned the conversation on its head, and announced he had a private party cabaret booking coming up onboard a ship moored off the south coast.

'I need a singer. In fact, I want you, and I'll pay well.' My talent buds were buried deep, and I said so. I admitted to him that my current musical career was confined to busking at Liverpool Street Station.

'That's fine. I still want you. We are playing for this Mexican politician, and the fee is four times the going rate.'

My mind wandered to bed number 157 on the second floor of the hostel – which was my lot – and I worried that any confidence I had of holding my own in showbiz bigtime had evaporated with the alcohol. Roger talked about his shows, and snippets entered my consciousness as I pondered the situation, '…the luxurious Hotel Hacienda Cocoyoc… President of Mexico… I'm far too modest to tell you how many lovers I had.'

I looked at Roger, just to see the smile on his face, in the hope it would bring inspiration into the hopelessness I felt, and the opportunities I had lost. Instead, his expression was wistful at best. I considered the possibility that getting well paid wasn't everything in life, and it made me think of Ginger. I had lost everything I ever had due to alcohol, and it had even influenced my decision regarding her. Defeating it and finding a way to help others do the same had become an obsession, which in itself had somewhat diluted my compulsion for the amber nectar. I remembered the words of C H Spurgeon, *'It was by perseverance, after all, that the snail reached the Ark.'*

'Okay, I'll do it.'

Roger's surprise was plain to see; he had probably given me up as a lost cause. 'But what will I do for clothes?' I asked. He jumped to his feet, startling me for an instant, 'Tomorrow is Saturday. I'll meet you here at 11am, and we'll get you all you need. Is that fair enough?' I nodded, somewhat dazed.

'When's the booking?' I enquired as though it was inconsequential.

'Saturday week,' he replied instantly, 'Plenty of time to plan.' I was glad he thought so. Suddenly, he went silent and it seemed as though someone had turned off a switch.

As much as a minute went by before I fully realised the fact, but when I did, the lack of conversation from his end made it stunningly obvious he was deep in thought. I was lost as to know how to handle it, and just when I was about to ask him if he had changed his mind, he continued in a low voice, gazing into space.

'I know what anxiety, depression, and psychiatric disorders are all about,' he said.

There was a large electric clock on the wall in the restaurant, and the story I heard when I was washing up was that it once stood on Liverpool Street mainline station. I sat watching the seconds hand ticking away as it circled the clockface. It did so twice before he spoke again.

'No matter what the root of your problem is, Nick, there will always be someone, somewhere, worse off than you are.' This time, the seconds hand circled three times before he continued, and while I knew Roger well enough to know he was leading up to something, the fact it was important to him too was obvious. So I waited patiently.

'My father was a wealthy man,' Roger managed a smile before he proceeded, but if there was a message behind the words, I was yet to pick it up, 'he owned a chocolate factory in Birmingham, and was also a show business agent. He put acts into various places, including the Birmingham Hippodrome. He met many superstars of the day and brought some of them home to parties and occasionally to stay. I remember having dinner at home with Hollywood legends Laurel and Hardy, and sitting on George Formby's knee while he sang to me at our house.'

I was amazed and in awe; these seemed to be amazing experiences and happy memories too, and I pondered on where his reference to anxiety, depression, and psychiatric disorders might kick in. Roger's voice resumed evenly.

'These happy times only occurred for me during school holidays because I attended a private boarding school in London which I learned to hate. The only good times I recall here, in the south, were the days when I could escape to the city and watch the Household Cavalry come and go from their Hyde Park Barracks.

'I dreamt of the day when I could join the regiment and parade alongside them, and eventually I did, but not before the devil struck an evil blow just before my tenth birthday.'

This time the pause was even longer, and I tired of watching the clock and just waited. When the words came, they did so with an enormous impact.

'One day, my mother came to the school to visit me unexpectedly and not at a normally scheduled time. I was called out of class and taken to where she sat alone – ashen-faced – in a small but comfortable room. There was no usual gushing welcome or hug, and I noticed her eyes were red and stained from crying.

'I'm afraid there is no easy way to tell you this, Roger,' she said in a tone which cracked and was unfamiliar to me, 'but I'm afraid your father has been charged with the murder of a young actress friend of his. He has to face a trial.'

'The words didn't register straight away,' continued Roger, 'my mother's voice droned on indecipherably in the ether. All I could think of were exciting times I had spent with a handsome father who could do no wrong. I barely remember her leaving me that day; only a teacher taking her place next to me and making a pledge that the school would do their utmost to keep the news away from my fellow pupils.

'Despite any efforts the staff may have made, it was inevitable the news would become common knowledge, and murder in those days came with the death penalty. One day, a national newspaper was left on my dormitory bed bearing a headline next to a large picture of my father. *Company Director Sentenced to Death* and someone had drawn a rope noose in pencil.

'My childhood was never the same again. Torment isn't a strong enough word to describe my plight. I was taken away from the school at some stage, but how long afterwards I have no idea, and I didn't return to mainstream school immediately. I have hazy memories of traipsing the streets of the town where we lived, with my mother, knocking door after door with a petition for clemency which would eventually go to the Home Secretary. She collected thousands of signatures and – thanks to her – his sentence was commuted to life in prison and he served about seven years. He never came home again, and I don't know any details as to why not, but it would be a long time before we met once more.'

In the silence, my eyes drifted back to the old railway station clock. Then Roger's voice regained my attention.

'I'm not interested in *why* you drink, Nick, and I have no suggestions on *how* to deal with such a problem anyway. I just wanted you to know that whatever it is, it can't be any worse than that!'

I nodded, but not in agreement. I was acknowledging to myself that I felt he was putting me down, or at best playing down the disease of alcohol dependency. Then the realisation hit home that my complaint was only one of many issues that had to be dealt with along life's highway, and I felt at the very least his equal. So I reached out instead and briefly gripped his hand.

*

'Shall we eat?' asked Roger, 'I'm paying.'

I screwed up my face with what was intended to demonstrate regret that I had no money. Roger called for a menu.

'How much is the gig worth?' I tried not to sound ungrateful or mercenary, and in fact, I was only pondering on whether to do it for free as a gesture.

'Yes, I want to talk to you about money.' Roger's tone suggested there was more good news to come, although I doubted it. 'Your mum was always good to me, Nick, and your dad too,' he spoke the words in almost a whisper 'but especially your Mum. She would always loan me some money when I was short, put girlfriends up for the night more than once, and I haven't forgotten that you subbed me too in better days.'

I wasn't going to deny it, more than once I'd done so when he was in a financial mess, and it reminded me I hadn't always been a failure.

'Are you going to take me out of my money misery, Rog?' He went silent for the first time in a while.

'I want to give you a bit of a break, Nick, all things considered. I'm probably one of the few who think you deserve a leg up, and after paying the orchestra for the gig, I'm left with two grand. I'll pay you a thousand to get you back on your feet again, providing you promise you will try your best to beat this thing.'

I was stunned!

'That's a deposit on a house,' I said.

He smiled and then added, 'You've got to pay me for the clothes out of it, though, is that okay?'

'Of course!' I answered, 'That's very generous of you Roger!'

'No booze, or the deal's off!' he said finally and didn't wait for a response. I just nodded.

*

Lunch became an enjoyable mix of discussions about old times, general chitchat, and an excellent meal. Roger explained how the upcoming gig came together, and more about the host – a Mexican politician who was now some sort of trade envoy – and we discussed what songs I would perform. Roger also chimed in with another carrot. "I've got a Fender copy guitar, a 100-watt amp, and a Marshall PA system with an equaliser and echo unit." The idea of playing with such first-rate equipment rekindled something inside me, and I could feel Nick Charles – the musician – bubbling up with excitement.

Later, after dessert was polished off, and Roger had picked up the tab, we parted ways. 'See you here, at 11am,' I confirmed as I turned and walked down the road. In less than a fortnight, I was going to play a gleaming Greek passenger yacht to more than 100 dignitaries and celebrities – something that was a million miles from what I expected when I awoke that morning. In the meantime, of course, I would return to bed number 157 at the Salvation Army Hostel for the homeless, in Petticoat Lane.

16: FACING THE DOC

'Good morning Doc, I know I'm a little early, but I've got to talk to you.'

Dr Weiser looked up from The Times crossword, which seemed a little out of place given his surroundings, and gave me a broad smile. 'It will be a pleasure, indeed,' he replied as I plugged in the kettle. I hoped he would still think so when I told him the news.

We sat with our mugs of tea steaming in the cold atmosphere of his surgery office, which his twin-bar electric fire had yet to adequately deal with, and I described my meeting with Roger. His smile was quickly replaced by a sad and then grim expression.

'I think we both know what this means, Nick. I suppose I had better put a lecture of my own together, don't you?' I leaned forward slowly and uttered words I meant from the bottom of my heart.

'I swear I won't touch a drink, Doc. I know I told you I hadn't finished drinking, but that's a kind of sixth sense instinct which lives inside me and I cannot explain it. But I *know* this isn't the time.'

He seemed to rally a little and even more so when I told him Roger would not pay me if I had a drink. I then outlined the morning's arrangements and the 11am appointment to go clothes buying, and he understood I would have to leave soon. Just the same, there was an odd feeling in the atmosphere when I departed, despite assurances I would see him later.

I had decided to arrive five minutes early to meet Roger, and felt an unfathomable sensation of relief when he arrived more or less on time.

Following friendly formalities, he shoved a piece of paper into my hand with the words, 'I think it's close enough to walk.' I noted the address of what I knew to be a fashionable gents clothing store, and he was right. The distance seemed nothing at all as we talked about old times and laughed at amusing anecdotes from days gone by.

The shop itself was quiet, and in a way of commanding a situation as only he could, Roger announced we needed a blue silk shirt and white trousers, white socks and shoes, a suit, two appropriate sports shirts, a further pair of smart shoes, dark socks to match, and a pack of briefs.

I hadn't an ounce of fat on me and everything came off the peg. I was impressed by the fact that casual male street fashion of the time could easily pass as stage gear, and the suit was an added and pleasant surprise.

The washing facilities at the hostel were hopelessly inadequate – bordering on useless – and so I had arisen before daybreak and suffered a strip wash alone in the freezing cold. I then adjourned to a one-woman launderette I knew a few hundred yards away, and sat in my underpants while she attempted a minor miracle on my tatty street clothes. She did her best, then tossed me a pair of second-hand but laundered briefs, and having signalled for me to change, threw my tattered ones into a waste bin.

At the front of my mind was how alcohol – in the quantities I consumed it – induced an almost subhuman, primaeval existence that eliminated the civilised requirement of personal hygiene. At least my recent period of sobriety had restored this, together with common decency, and I had spared myself the ultimate indignity of appearing thus in front of Roger. However, the ragged clothes spoke for themselves.

Nevertheless, he wasn't stupid, and without consultation he ordered a further pair of casual trousers, two spare shirts, and tossed a few extra pairs of socks and briefs onto the mounting pile. I wasn't going to pick up a grand for the gig that was for sure, but there was a quiet satisfaction in the knowledge I would pay for these in a week's time.

'I'll leave you with some spare underwear and socks, Nick, but I think the rest will be safer with me until next weekend. I suspect wardrobe space will be at a bit of a premium where you're staying at the moment.' His words stung a bit, and I could have told him there was plenty of space at the Doc's, but I didn't. He had to keep another appointment, and so we parted with a firm handshake and an arrangement for our first rehearsal in a lifetime to take place the following day.

*

The rehearsals were held at a studio in North London. They included a friendly and proficient drummer, and we worked well together from the start. Roger commented that I had improved more than he could have hoped for. Me?!? I wasn't so sure. I was familiar with the equipment, and it didn't take long before busking seemed a distant memory; just the same, a life of alcoholic destruction had left a mark on my confidence.

I had nothing new to learn and remembered by heart all the lyrics of the songs I was to perform. As first agreed, my contribution was to be a pop-cum-rock medley, and we worked out segues in seconds. One exception was in the middle of it, when a musical tacet presented the opportunity for me to tell a tale or two of life on the road with Roger in the early years.

We both agreed after three sessions, the last of which was on the Wednesday afternoon, that we were good to go. Roger handed over a smart case prior to my departure, informing me it contained the balance of my new clothes, and walked with me to the nearest tube station. His parting words were, 'Do not let me down, Nick!' And he emphasised every syllable!

I stored my new case at the Doc's surgery and continued with the construction of the lecture I was working on with him, and Roger rang so frequently to check on me that they even got to talk and laugh together like friends.

Saturday came quickly and with it a sick feeling. The plan was for me to be at the surgery at the usual time; there were adequate washing facilities and my clothes were already there, and the Doc would be a steadying influence. He assured me 'sufficient butterflies to set up a lepidopterarium' was a healthy sign, and would keep me on my toes. I had never heard of such a thing, so he explained that it was a facility specifically intended for the breeding and display of butterflies. We both laughed a lot at that, and as it kept cropping up, it proved to take the edge off the nervousness I felt. Finally, I was dressed neatly in my new casual clothes and it was soon time to meet with Roger.

I had no wish to be collected from the hostel and so we had agreed to meet mid-morning outside the café restaurant where we had recently eaten, although it seemed an age ago. He introduced me to Terry who was sat in his van's passenger seat as our drummer for the evening, paying huge compliments to Terry's playing ability, and then did the same to Terry in respect of me. The van was only small, packed solid, and had what appeared to be a narrow pull-up passenger seat in the rear, which I assumed would be mine. Roger pointed to it.

'I'm going to sit there, and you can drive; it will be quite like old times, except this time you will be licensed and insured.' I was surprised as Roger was over six foot tall, and it was not going to be a comfortable journey for him. I was about to say something to this effect when Terry spoke instead.

'Roger will be fine, Nick. He likes to kip to the sound of the engine.' It wasn't like the Roger I knew, although in those distant days I did do a great deal of the driving and had never given it a thought. Terry got out and pulled the front seat forward for Roger to squeeze in, and I got behind the wheel. With Terry settled back, he passed me a large atlas followed by the words, 'You'd better take a look at this, Nick.' I did so but pretty much knew the way and turned around in the road when a gap presented itself. We were on our way!

It proved to be an uneventful trip. We stopped twice, mainly for Roger to stretch his legs which only served to question his decision of taking the tiny seating space, although we did have coffees at each service station.

I knew we had plenty of time, so I had taken a leisurely drive, and we were slowed down further by roadworks. As a result, it took almost three hours to complete the journey. By the time we had located the passenger yacht and Roger's contact, it was after 3pm, and we were pleased when we eventually got aboard with our equipment. Fortunately, there were helpers on hand who were already busy with the orchestra's equipment and props, and for a while it was frantic. Eventually, everything calmed down and I had time to explore the boat. I was attempting to see if access to the Ship's Bridge was possible when Roger's contact – whose name was Harry – beckoned me from a lower level and offered to show me the cabin allotted for a changing room.

I'm not sure what I was expecting. In fact, I had barely given the matter a thought, but when I saw it, I was truly impressed. It was much larger than I would have imagined a cabin to be, and it had an ensuite bathroom and toilet. The bedroom itself stretched to a lounge-type seating area and it had been recently decorated. My guitar for the night was leaning up against one of the club chairs and, by their absence, I guessed the rest of the equipment had been set up in the concert room. It transpired Harry's next task was to take me there, and I was greeted by a surprising sight.

The concert room was almost the width of the liner, and the length was perhaps 20 feet longer. Before me, an extraordinary cosmetic change was taking place as a small army of what you might describe as scene shifters were erecting sections that were slowly taking the shape of 1960's Flower Power London. An impressive lighting system – which included a bank, super trooper and other static special effects units – was also being strategically placed. Just then, Roger appeared and I greeted him in astonishment.

'My God, Rog, this lot must be costing a small fortune, and all for one night. Did you know about all this?' He shook his head with a wry grin on his face.

'All our stuff is set up by the looks of things,' I noted. 'Why don't we do a soundcheck while we have the chance?' I looked towards the medium-sized grand piano which had the lid propped up, and two microphones set high and (in my view) too far back. 'Why don't you put your head together with the orchestra keyboard player and see what he thinks. I don't like the look of the way they've got that lot set up.'

Roger nodded, 'I'll go and see him now,' he said and walked away hurriedly. It took me less than fifteen minutes to set my share up, by which time I noticed Terry in conference with his opposite number drummer. The outcome of this was they both agreed to use the orchestra's drums to save space, and Terry actually looked pleased.

There was a large lounge with a bar set aside for us musicians, and once changed into our stage finery, we gathered there happily and talked shop. I knew Roger's Mexican trade envoy pal would make himself known at some point, and when he did, I was not disappointed. He was an educated gentleman and a lovable rogue with a mischievous twinkle in his eyes, and for the fleeting of moments when something went wrong, I saw the Mexican bandit. There were also familiar famous faces, some from the acting profession and others not so well known but prominent in radio nonetheless.

I was pleased to meet a well-known film producer who, like me, was drinking lemonade. He said he was an alcoholic, four years dry, and wanted to know what my excuse was… I told him I was too, but could only lay claim to a few months. He advised me to keep going to the meetings, and I found it hard to refrain from telling him that if that was all there was to help me, I'd throw myself under a bus!

The night turned out very successfully all round. The audience was far bigger than we had expected, and the concert room was packed; clearly, the theme had been carefully planned, and Flower Power was depicted in dress by all and sundry. The orchestra started out traditionally, but as the evening progressed, it was obvious the crowd wanted fun, and so they switched neatly to more of a big band presentation. I would have given them nine out of ten if asked and then only because nothing is perfect. Roger was outstanding and as good as I had ever seen him (I gave him nine and a half). As for myself, I was completely sober and, therefore, a more able critic; I decided seven out of ten was about right. Not bad for a street busker masquerading in the big time.

It is hard to describe the sober reaction of someone who has imbibed for a lifetime, seeing the slow but sure inebriation of others taking place before them. It struck me as deterioration. Too often, I've found it truly disturbing when delightful people behave outrageously out of character, yet few recall anything awry the following day. I decided it would provide a journey of enlightenment to advocate in my work – the theory that everyone should attend a party at least once in their lifetime alcohol-free. Just to observe the madness! On the streets, I have witnessed barbarous acts and some I prefer not to record. As far as this trip was concerned, nothing was going to tempt me to drink. I saw it as a wonderful opportunity to gather material for my carrier bags, and provide yet another parable… as the Doc called them. Thankfully, there had been no sign whatsoever of the call of the wild.

We stayed late afterwards and Roger spent much of it with his envoy pal; for the most part, they were in deep conversation. Terry and I enjoyed most of this time chatting to each other and with others who joined us from time to time. He had worked with some of the biggest names in the business as a session drummer, and I knew from the moment he had struck a skin that he was special. Some of the stories he told had me in stitches. It only got serious when he asked about my drinking, and so I didn't labour it, although he did try hard to get me to open up. I guessed Roger had told him of bed 157.

At 3am, we set off back to London at a steady pace, and as they both slept for most of it, little was said. Our Mexican host had offered all three of us hotel accommodation for the night; however, Roger needed to be back in London for some obscure reason, so we declined. I didn't reveal I would be unable to get access to the hostel until 7am.

We arrived all too soon for me, and I turned the van around in an unusually deserted Bishopsgate at Roger's request. 'It'll save me doing it,' he said as Terry allowed him out of his cramped position to take over behind the wheel. Before doing so, he gave me a sealed envelope with the words, 'Don't waste a penny of it.'

'What about the clothes?' I asked, referring to the money I owed him.

'Forget it. You did brilliantly tonight, and you got me out of a big hole.'

It was too early in the morning to crack a joke about me being in the hole, and so I shook his hand warmly and instead commented, 'I think that definitely makes us even, Rog.' As he departed, he gave me a card and told me to keep in touch.

I watched them disappear into the distance and headed towards where there might be people, and therefore safety in numbers. On the way, a group of hard-case vagrant drunks, stumbling along on the opposite side of the road, hurled insults in my direction.

I wondered how pleased they would have been to see me had they known I had a thousand pounds in my back trouser pocket.

17: LECTURE DAYS

The Doc was pleased to see me but not excessively. When I reminded him that since leaving his surgery I had been surrounded by booze for several hours, taken part in a significant cabaret, and returned alcohol-free, he simply replied, 'I am more concerned by how you will react next time you feel the call of the wild.' I did not comment.

He had a point because I knew I hadn't had my last drink but – as of that moment – I didn't know why. Of one thing I had no doubt, though, I had to open a bank account and pay in my £1,000. I retrieved the envelope from my pocket and placed it in front of him.

'Can you help me open a bank account so I can get rid of this?' I asked.

He opened it and gasped, counted it, and then gasped again, then with a smile he said, 'We go now.'

The process was completed in no time at all. He was known and well-respected at the bank, and they accepted the surgery as my temporary address and were happy to provide me with a chequebook. I kept twenty pounds back, which gave me a little independence at least.

Back at the surgery, the Doc suggested I should write an introductory passage for the lecture. He told me to make it impactive and emphasised the importance of grabbing their attention straight away, so I buried myself in the task of searching through my research notes for something suitable. The Doc did paperwork too, and there was little said between us. I beavered away searching through hundreds of loose pages and also exercise books, often unable to read my scribble. I could easily distinguish between reasoned out useful observations and drunken ramblings, yet oddly it was the latter which provided much food for thought.

We lunched together, as usual, and it was while walking to his favourite eating place that he confided how he had not slept during my night away. Having unburdened himself in me, he shook his head as a horse might do – although in his case. I think it was an attempt to clear his head of the memory – and I felt an indefinable sense of guilt.

By the end of the day, I hadn't really achieved what I had set out to do and felt a shade disappointed and told him so. Before he could respond, I assured him – with a grin – that I would overcome the stumbling blocks and come up with a masterpiece! We both laughed at this, and finally I felt he was back to his normal self, and soon afterwards we parted for the day.

*

Much later, the distant church clock which had often been a friend, as well as a tormentor, chimed 2am. I sat up in my dormitory bed and listened to the sounds of the dozens of disturbed souls lying around me while considering the task ahead. I eased myself out of Bed 157, walked to the concrete staircase and sat on the top stone step. A sudden thought occurred to me. If I was right, and our forthcoming audiences would lack a real grasp of the complexities of alcohol addiction, perhaps I should begin with a bit of my own real-life drama.

The distant clock struck the single blow of the quarter-hour, and as it did so, I retrieved an A4 writing pad from its refuge beneath the mattress of my bed and returned to the top stair. This time I had my pillow to sit on and took a deep breath as I started to write.

'A New Dawn in the Approach to Alcohol Dependency'

For a victim, there is nothing louder than the sound of the alcohol-dependent heart beating in the dead of night. Without their drink, and in withdrawal, they lie in pain, begging for their greatest love to return.

There is nothing more depressing than the thought the next generation of alcohol dependents will come from our children. It is their right to know of the dangers of abusing alcohol and it is *our* duty to ensure they do so.

No child should grow up in the insanity of an alcohol-abusing household. Even parents who think their drinking is normal are often divorced from reality, and then all too frequently from each other!

Then, they watch their children travel the same road from their respective directions and they feel no blame, but then why should they? No one told them of the dangers either. We have to put this right by addressing the alcohol problem as a whole.

The blame must lie somewhere, and perhaps communities themselves have much to answer for, because too many see no harm in copious amounts of alcohol. Society likes to drink.

The fight against the complexities of alcohol dependency takes us on a long, winding, and intricate road. It is utter misery to navigate and impossible to resurface. Alcohol's conscience is as cold as a witch's heart.

Dr Weiser and I may provide the very last stopping place on a voyage too many of your patients may already be taking. And with few ways back.

I invite you to join me on a journey of discovery, often through rough waters, and witness hell on earth. For many of your patients, their only lifebelt could be you. And together, we must keep an eye on the next generation.

This episode begins in a hospital where I found myself with no recollections of how I came to be there. I was sat up in bed reading an article in a magazine about Joseph Goebbels, Adolf Hitler's wartime propaganda minister. It was said, had he not been known for all the wrong reasons, he would have probably gone down in history as being the greatest public relations man the world had ever known. It went on to describe how he had mesmerised a nation into believing an illusion.

I remember putting down the magazine and gazing at a blank wall opposite me, thinking of the strength and depth of the alcohol illusion and delusion under which I had spent so much of my life. Its strength and intensity was such that, despite this, the very thought of being lost to its foul grip, filled me with misery. Abruptly, a hospital doctor's voice interrupted my thoughts.

'You can carry on drinking alcohol as you are doing right now and *die within a month*, or stop completely *and have a life.*'

*

It had become my usual practice to walk to Dr Weiser's surgery the long way round, and he was usually in situ when I arrived. On this occasion, I was extra early and he was nowhere to be seen. I really had no idea what time he arrived and had never thought to ask him. It was with considerable relief I saw him in the distance approaching with his customary carry case, and as he got closer he gave me a cheery wave.

'Are you ready to have another go at the lecture introduction, Nick?'

I held up the A4 pad. He stopped in his tracks and put his case down onto the dusty pavement. Well, I wasn't expecting that. I really wasn't.' His surprise was genuine.

The Doc unlocked the surgery door and entered with me close behind. I put the kettle on while he did his usual wrestle with his inefficient twin-bar electric fire. With tea made and the small fire having proved it was slightly more useful than it looked, he took up his familiar position and looked in my direction expectantly.

'Are you ready?' I asked him, already knowing the answer.

'Of course,' he replied with a grin.

Comfortably seated, I read my late-night introduction from my A4 pad. I took my time and did my best to hit every beat and point fittingly, and when I finally stopped my narration, I looked up at the Doc.

'What do you think Doc?'

I am not sure what I expected. In fact, it had never entered my head to receive anything other than calm approval or gentle criticism. I certainly did not expect to see tears in his eyes and witness him swallowing hard to fight back his emotions. For several seconds, there was an awkward silence, I didn't know what to say and seemingly he couldn't find words either. Just when I was going to suggest we went for breakfast – for want of something better to verbalise – he burst into laughter.

'I knew you could do it, my boy. I'm a silly old man, but I found it quite moving to hear my scruffy, homeless street drinking protégé compose words no university or medical school would have the knowledge to provide.'

Now it was my turn to be emotional, and it welled up inside of me, making it hard to swallow despite the necessity to do so. The Doc then came to my rescue, and I was grateful he did.

'C'mon, let's go for breakfast.' He had a huge smile almost distracting my attention from his red eyes, and I followed him out through the ancient, battered door, which he turned and locked as though it was a precious jewel box. In that moment, I understood the true meaning of vocation.

*

The run-up to our six-week lecture series passed surprisingly quickly. Two of the talks would be for the benefit of hospital medical staff. Two were invited audiences of GPs, and the remaining two were a mixture of psychiatric nurses, probation officers, social workers, and others working in the field of troubled souls.

'How do we get there?' I enquired while scanning the list of venues during lunch the day before the inaugural lecture performance.

'I've got a car,' replied the Doc, ignoring my surprise, 'And you can drive it,' he added, almost as an afterthought.

At day's end, we parted, conceding that we were a shade nervous, which I suspect was an understatement for both of us. We offered each other mini-pep talks that ended in laughter as a result of their inaptness and then separated somewhat later than usual.

The following morning, I bumped into the man with the wake-up whistle as he left reception, holding it poised to wake the inmates to face yet another day of misery. I hadn't been able to sleep and tossed and turned all night. I rose early and decided to walk for an hour and then wait outside the surgery for the Doc to arrive.

London Bridge was my destination and having dallied for a while, I headed back and stopped for a coffee on my way to the surgery. As I rounded the final corner, it was to witness the most extraordinary sight.

A black French Citroën Traction Avant saloon car, the vehicle most favoured by the Gestapo in WW2 to carry squads of their goons, and the mere sight of which terrorised the population, came careering towards me.

It wasn't that it was travelling at high speed; it was just that it seemed completely out of control! It was going up and down like a rider on a rodeo horse, and veered from one side of the road to the other violently. Finally, it skidded to a tyre-shrieking halt outside the surgery – although nearer the middle of the road than the kerb – and out struggled the familiar shape of the Doc! I ran anxiously towards him as he leaned with his back against the car, and asked him if he was alright.

'Oh, my dear God. I never could master the damn gears,' he said, wiping his brow with an immaculate white linen handkerchief taken from the chest pocket of an immaculate suit.

I took the keys from him, 'Why don't I park it for you?' He nodded and moved away from the car. 'How far have you come?' I added.

'Ten miles,' he muttered as I followed him into his premises.

'Ye Gods,' was the best I could manage.

I drove the car each day for our series of lectures and enjoyed every moment. At the talks, we could not have wished for a better outcome to our efforts, and I knew I looked good in the suit Roger had bought me. It was when we met at his surgery the day after our final lecture presentation that the Doc delivered some devastating news.

I knew there was something wrong the moment he opened and read a letter which had been delivered by hand. He placed it down on his desk in front of him, and there was a troubled look on his face.

'I'm afraid we have to leave the premises this week, Nick,' he explained, painfully shoving the letter towards me.

I looked down at it, numbed by the reality. It didn't take a genius to work out that our part of London was slowly being demolished and rebuilt, and that our building was one of the last standing locally. The letter was simply the death notice.

'In my naivety, I thought they would give me alternative premises… such is the need. Now I come to think about it, once all of this has gone, even the vagrant community will have to find rubble and condemned property elsewhere.' The Doc looked at me, utterly overcome. I felt similarly devastated whenever I succumbed to alcohol having enjoyed a period of sobriety. It was different, yet it was the same; a defeat to be vanquished. This was simply another version.

'What will you do now, Doc?' I asked, knowing he would have no answer, but feeling I needed to pose the question all the same.

'I don't know, Nick. There are very few answers available for those who have fallen on the alcohol battlefield. Perhaps, one day, you will find a way. I think we are both in God's hands now, my boy.'

It was the first time I had heard him utter anything religious, and I thought about his Eastern European accent and the Citroën car he owned. The question I asked was inevitable.

'Are you Jewish, Doc?'

'Yes, an Austrian Jew.' He paused. 'I survived a Nazi concentration camp, but only just. I was more use to them as a doctor than a corpse.' He halted once more, 'I survived to keep others alive and working. I am pleased to say, as a result, many others lived too, and for this I thank my God.'

'And the Gestapo's favourite car?'

He smiled an inscrutable smile and then cleared up any doubt with his reply. 'The fear generated by the very sight and distinctive sound of that dreaded vehicle was felt by tens of thousands. Following the war, I had constant nightmare reruns of when I was hauled into one, and taken to Nazi headquarters for questioning. The nightmares only stopped when I bought such a car and tried to make it my friend. As you will have noticed, I did not entirely succeed.' I tried not to smile, but I did just the same.

'You might say fate has now struck you another deadly blow, Doc?' I wondered precisely what he was thinking at that moment. I doubted his reply summed it up.

'God moves in a mysterious way,' was all he said.

*

The next few days were frenetic. A last-minute appeal failed mainly on the grounds that the Doc was beyond retirement age, and therefore the Local Authority could not justify the investment. They very much doubted any qualified doctor would want to inherit the load in the future. In addition to this, a new domestic building programme was scheduled as well as a tourist centre; the requirement would be for a modern medical centre and drunken vagrants would not be welcome.

On the Wednesday, a transit van arrived and together with the driver, the Doc and I loaded it with all he wished to keep. Then, we had a last lunch together at his favourite restaurant. He asked me to keep him up-to-date with what happened to as many of his vagrant patients as I could, and promised to contact me by leaving a message at the hostel reception. Later, he waved through the side passenger window of the van until it turned out of sight.

I stood at the surgery, all by myself, for the final time. In a moment of sheer maddening frustration, I kicked the surgery door as hard as I could, and it caved in off its hinges. A sudden pang of conscience made me turn to see if my act of vandalism had been witnessed, and indeed there *were* people around, going about their everyday affairs.

But nobody had noticed. Nobody cared.

18: THE NEW DAWN

When I was eight years old, and at Primary School, a new boy started who had moved to the Midlands from Devon. His name was Gordon, and while he seemed a delightful character, he was slightly eccentric, which I didn't understand. In some ways, he was extremely intelligent, and in others, he was not on the same wavelength as the rest of us. The Headmaster, Mr Wilkins, gave me the task of helping Gordon settle in. We weren't best friends (mine was Paul), and as there was an odd number of boys in the class, Gordon sat alone. Nonetheless, the seeds were planted for a lifelong friendship.

Different types of bullying existed, as with most schools. Some were mental, others physical; Gordon was a victim, and so was I. When he was thirteen, he transferred to another school because of the bullying, but I had less choice and weathered the storm. One particular bully was to have a significant effect on my life…

I had a scar on the end of my nose, which Mum told me was a minor wound caused by forceps during delivery. The subject was taboo in our household and rarely referred to, and it took a conversation in later years with a lifelong friend of my mother's to reveal its true origin. Apparently, the truth is that I was born with a birthmark-type growth on the tip of my nose, and it had to be removed in order to avoid it becoming unsightly. It was during this procedure that the medics discovered the roots of it ran deep and – in order to prevent a re-emergence – it became a major operation. Fortunately, my surgeon had worked with Sir Archibald McIndoe, the famous WWII plastic surgeon, and he did a wonderful job. The downside was that nerves normally protected by tissue were left exposed beneath the skin and the legacy was the slightest knock caused me excruciating and indescribable pain. I consider the occasional agonising experience a cheap price to pay, but there were extremely humiliating and embarrassing events along the way which haunt me still.

When it was my turn to be picked on by the aforementioned school bully, he hit me hard dead centre on the operation scar, and I screamed in agony and sobbed for far longer than could ever have been seen as reasonable. God only knows what teachers and fellow pupils thought of this pathetic child but then, of course, they didn't know! It is therefore inexplicable that I should have volunteered for boxing when it was introduced in the Scout Troop to which I was a member. Pip, who was now my best friend, was my nominated opponent and the very first thing he did was hit me on the nose… and I completely lost it! In agonising pain, I showered him with totally unnecessary blows as brutal as I was capable of delivering, and it haunts me to this day. There was a personal price to pay, he ceased to be my best friend, and I left the Scouts voluntarily and in personal ignominy shortly afterwards.

It would be hard to imagine any good coming out of my alcoholism. However, if there was, it had to be its anaesthesia which either deadened the pain in my nose, or robbed me of the memory of many hand to hand skirmishes on the alcohol battlefield.

It was destined that Gordon and I would meet periodically throughout our lives and often in what I would describe as times of need. The first of these (post-school) was when I rounded a corner with a girlfriend in my clapped-out old Hillman motor car, and spotted him pushing an even more dilapidated pre-war convertible relic. I stopped to help, and we discussed our respective progress in life, and how we intended to become millionaires.

By the time I was twenty-two, I was unemployable due to alcohol, and one day bumped into him outside a betting office in the town. Somehow, he was different – on edge – talking gibberish about cleaning out the bookies with a new gambling system he had perfected, and he looked as scruffy as I did. As we talked, he admitted to being homeless and I offered him temporary accommodation, which he gratefully accepted.

I was now married to my first wife with a young daughter and the relationship was hanging by a thread. We lived in a hovel of the type that drunken wastrels occupied. I deserved it; mother and daughter did not. One day, she realised it and sought pastures new. Then, unexpectedly, I was offered a two-year contract to work second-rate musical bookings, and I took Gordon with me as a roadie. Somewhere along the line, he went his own way and so did I, but mine was for failing to turn up for shows and destitution beckoned.

'Hello, Gordon.' I don't remember saying the words; he told me of them later. I had regained consciousness on a bench outside the SS in Stepney, and slowly he materialised amongst a sea of vagrant faces. He was conspicuous by the fact he was wearing an evening dress suit and stuck out like a sore thumb.

'Where's the Doc?' I asked him, unable to think clearly and then turned to wondering if I had missed a lesson at school.

'Who's the Doc?' Gordon looked concerned.

'Where's your old car?' I asked, ignoring his question.

'C'mon, I'll buy you a coffee,' he replied.

My memory partially returned with the coffee, although Gordon's appearance was more difficult to grasp.

Before Gordon's manifestation, several weeks had passed with no messages from the Doc and no one could tell me where he could be found. I'd asked the staff at the hostel and they knew nothing. My last conscious recollection, prior to Gordon, was standing in a queue at the bank and then another in a busy London lunchtime pub. There was no call of the wild, just an insane urge to be under the influence of the most dangerous drug known to man. Gordon's voice sounded again.

'I've got a job as a waiter. It's at a plush gentleman's club; the money's good, and from next week I can live-in. I could get you a job if you want it?' His voice droned on and I sat drinking the coffee, and then he bought some more and I drank that too. Slowly, sense and reason returned.

*

I had never waited silver service, and had to rely on Gordon's know-how to learn. He also knew of a second-hand clothing store that had a section specialising in dress suits for city waiters at all levels. So I relied on his generosity to provide me with evening dress, a necessity for the silver service waiter.

It emerged Gordon had become a compulsive gambler (the addiction side of which was something I could identify with), and he'd lost everything as indeed had I. How it came about, I'm unsure, but we made a pact which amounted to 'he wouldn't gamble' if I 'didn't drink', and vice versa. We both felt if we could achieve a year, we would have broken the backs of our respective addictions. A month later, I saw him coming out of a betting shop and we had words; it ended with him returning to his home county in the south-west.

I stayed on at the club and just before my birthday, and with ten months of sobriety under my belt, I felt confident enough to ring my mother and tell her I'd beaten my evil foe. My father answered the phone.

'I'm sorry, Nick. She'd had a great deal of worry and it affected her brain. She had suffered some sort of dementia and your sister and I suffered alongside her. I'm afraid she walked in front of a car and it ended her life. The funeral…'

The rest of his words were lost. I recall running and sobbing until I could do so no longer, and then collapsing onto a pavement and people milling around. I recollect pushing them away, then entering a bar and drinking to forget, until I awoke in a hospital bed and remembered.

It seemed I had sustained some worrying injuries in a fight during which I had been stabbed. It was not a life-threatening wound, but a consultant was concerned about swelling and bruising in my liver region. A nurse told me it had been necessary to clean me up before they could tell bruise from dirt, and I was ashamed.

Such are the mysteries of the alcoholic's grapevine that my old AA Meeting friend, Frank, heard about my demise and visited me in hospital. His first words were, 'What possessed you to have a drink after being sober for so many months, Nick?'

I explained my mother had been killed in a car accident.

'How is she?' he asked.

'She's bloody dead!' I spoke the words angrily. I was in no mood to treat fools gladly.

'So she didn't rise again when you drank the drink?'

Suddenly the impact and meaning behind his words registered. A long silence followed because I couldn't think of a reply and, of course, we both knew there wasn't one. Alcohol solved nothing.

The doctor was sufficiently concerned to send me for various tests, which is a tribute to him given I was clearly a vagrant, not just because of my appearance but I was also NFA – the abbreviation for No Fixed Abode.

I was hospitalised for two weeks, and then discharged in second-hand clothes plus a handout from a charity for wastrels like me. We bore the mark of destitution, were known to have nothing, and were never expected to have anything. Then I remembered my bank account.

As I was about to leave, a young woman called my name and came running towards me as I walked slowly towards the exit. She addressed me breathlessly.

'I was the night nurse on duty when you were admitted. The ambulance crew were given two carrier bags full of written work, and I put them in a locker for safety. They looked like important documents. If you come with me, I'll give them to you.' I must have looked at her vaguely.

'I can throw them in the incinerator if you prefer?' She looked hurt.

'Good God, no!' I managed, 'I'm sorry, I'm not quite with it yet!'

She took my arm supportively and led me along a labyrinth of corridors and down some stairs that seemed to lead to the basement. Finally, we arrived at a row of tall metal lockers and she opened the first one with a key. A nurse's uniform was in evidence, personal belongings and – on the floor of it – my two carrier bags.

'I hope you don't mind, but I took a quick look… I figured you might want them. I was afraid they might have been sent to the incinerator.'

I responded gratefully and at once. 'I'm so pleased it was you who found them; I can't thank you enough.'

My voice sounded hollow as it still reflected my most recent battle with the bottle.

'How are you feeling now?' she asked, as if reading my thoughts. 'You've had a bad time, haven't you?'

I nodded, and she took my arm again as we retraced our steps back to the street. An involuntary thought told me she was the sort of girl my mother would have liked me to marry.

For her part, she was entirely and vocationally professional and wished me well as she went her way. I waited until she was out of sight and then sat down on a bench to think.

Unexpectedly, I had a sudden urge to be with my own kind and decided to look for some of the Doc's patients. I got up, headed over to Spitalfields – via the bank – and discovered half a dozen of them around an open fire. As the demolition programme continued, they were rarely in the same place and moved almost every day and consequently became harder to find. The problem was a fire needed fuel and the only source was the market workers who donated the non-returnable wooden cases out of pity. I realised with mixed feelings that there would soon be an end to this sacred homeless icon too, and having found a group of six, I accepted the bottle being handed around before realising what I had done. I went to pass it on untouched, and then changed my mind and took a huge swig which drew derision from the gathering. I took some of the recently drawn money from my pocket and passed it to the man who owned the bottle. At once, everyone was happy.

It was dark when I opened my eyes and every movement was painful. It took an age to struggle into a sitting position and when I did so, I immediately slumped with my back against an old Victorian wall. I recognised the square space I was in, at the bottom of cellar steps, from a previous occasion when I had either fallen or been thrown down. This time there was a vile smell of urine, excrement, and the rotting corpse of a large rat. I fingered what appeared to be a deep gash in the side of my head, hidden by my long, thick hair and I became conscious that my front and side were covered in congealed blood. I ached everywhere and tried to stand. It took several minutes, but eventually I was upright and I painfully tried out various limbs expecting something to be broken. It wasn't until I rubbed my right eye in an attempt to ease bruising, that I felt a small piece of bone which I could move backwards and forwards through the skin. It was clearly a fracture in my eye socket, and I had no idea how long it had been like it.

There didn't seem to be any other fractures, and I set about climbing the litter-covered concrete stairs and eventually made it to the top. It revealed a miserable day, with the sort of drizzle which soaked a man unless he was already wet through (as I was), and I briefly considered the hospital. I thrust my hands into my pockets and felt the unmistakable sensation of money, the paper variety in one and coins in the other. The insane logic of the vagrant street drinker kicked in, and I headed for a licensed shop run by a scruffy man who didn't care what his customers looked or smelt like. His wall clock told me it was just after six o'clock, although I had already guessed it was morning. I ordered a bottle of brandy and was about to hand over the money when an extraordinary thing happened; I was overcome by an overwhelming urge to have a bath!

'I'll come back later,' I told the startled man, pushing the bottle back towards him and snatching up my money.

*

'If you stick your dirty clothes in this bag, I'll launder them while you take a bath.' The kindly cockney voice belonged to the lady who ran the public baths on the main road heading east out of London. It had taken an hour to walk there; not easy in my condition. I had used the facility a number of times, and I knew her face well. I'm not sure she remembered me, but I was welcomed like an old friend and it gave me a warm feeling. I took up her offer and relaxed in the piping hot water, stretching out like a wealthy industrialist might do in his South of France penthouse flat overlooking the Med. For a while, I imagined I was something I was not.

'C'mon darlin', the bloody water will be cold!' I emerged abruptly from a dead sleep and struggled to get out of the bath. Her voice wasn't authoritarian in any way. I believe she genuinely cared, and she quickly recognised my plight and offered a helping hand like a nurse in a hospital might do. The door closed behind her and I dried on a worn-through but warm bath towel, and then donned my carefully laundered and neatly-folded clothes. Underneath the final garment were several five and ten-pound notes and a pile of change, all neatly arranged as if in a gesture of honesty. She waved me off through the open door. I don't suppose she had many tips, and certainly never £20 from a homeless vagrant, especially at a moment in time when it was a week's wages for many people!

*

Historically, I had worked as a barman in many London pubs and got the sack from all of them for drunkenness. All except one. I walked to Trafalgar Square for no other reason than to sit and search my brain for sense and reason. An added attraction was that I often felt like I belonged to the human race when surrounded by tourists. There had been a busy lunchtime pub near Lambeth Bridge which Gordon had told me about, and where I had worked for a week during a sober spell. I was good at it when I didn't drink, and the manager, whose name I recalled was Bob, said he would give me a full-time job if ever I wanted one, and I could live-in to boot.

I headed off towards where it was situated on Horseferry Road, and sat on a bench near Westminster Hospital. It was hard to describe the feeling in my head, and the nearest I can is to say it was one of total commitment to change, almost spiritual. Big Ben struck 11am, and it seemed only shortly afterwards the quarter-hour; it was time to make personal history.

I stood up feeling good and determined in a way I had never previously experienced in my lifetime. The fact was, I knew I was about to take my very last drink of alcohol. This act was to kill a part of myself and undergo a kind of death. Alcohol was part of me, like another vitally important limb, and this symbolic mindset was the metaphorical signing of a sobriety covenant. There were no doubts in my mind, whatsoever; it would remain in place forever.

I crossed Horseferry Road and stepped off the pavement on the corner of Dean Bradley Street, just as a member of staff opened the doors for the day's business at The Marquis of Grandy, a pub I knew vaguely. Our eyes met briefly. His showed vague signs of recognition and for the right reasons, I hoped. I entered passing pleasantries and ordered a half-pint of bitter which he dispensed with a cheerful response, placing it on clean cloth matting. I studied it, searching the amber liquid for demons and signs of hell. I thought of vagrant friends and visualised their images in the glass attempting to swim to safety. In one moment of alcoholic madness, I restrained a powerful urge to reach into the glass and scoop them to safety. I had no such desire to prevent myself from reciting the words of Mario Savio out loud, and I did so without caring if anyone heard.

*'There is a time when the operation of the machine becomes so odious, makes you so sick at heart, you can't take part; you can't even tacitly take part, and you've got to put your bodies upon the gears and upon the wheels, upon the levers, upon all the apparatus... And you've just **got** to make it stop.'*

I drained the glass as Big Ben struck the half-hour and noticed a calendar on the wall behind the bar. I already knew it was 11.30am; I now knew it was December 13th 1976.

I would have thanked the barman for my very last drink, but he was making preparations for the day with lifting noises emanating from the cellar below. And so I departed with my thoughts from my nightmare life of embarrassment and destruction; a life which had lasted fourteen long years. I was alone except for my God.

I must have arrived at the Barley Mow at a crucial time because Bob, the manager, made me feel like the cavalry, and I soon found out why. Staff shortages had made it so difficult that apart from Maureen – an attractive and competent barmaid in her middle thirties – the rest were beginners. This was a recipe for mayhem in a chaotic bar that catered for hundreds of office workers between 12 and 2pm. The time fled, and once it was over, Bob called me to his office.

Guilt is a bedfellow for the sober alcoholic with a conscience. I knew I was not at my best, and I was worried my efforts had not been enough. Withdrawal from my latest drunken bender, the duration of which would remain forever unknown, had kicked in on the hour mark and detoxing as a barman is yet another nightmare. I knew that – outside of prescribed medication – the only thing capable of relieving the devastating mental and physical pain was another drink. The downside was all it would succeed in doing was to offer a temporary respite, making subsequent and inevitable withdrawal worse than ever. All that remained for me was to grit my teeth and work through it. As for Bob, I need not have worried, his reason for wanting to see me was to say how delighted he had been with my efforts, and his words proved to be a healthy tonic of sorts.

'The rush is over now,' he explained. 'I'll show you your room, and you can settle in. I'm afraid you will be sharing for the first week, but then your roommate will be going back to college. His name is David.' I thought momentarily of recent vagrant bedfellows, and smiled inwardly at the comparison between them and David, who he described as a student-teacher. 'You'll like him, he's a nice lad,' Bob added almost as an afterthought.

*

Bob had put me on a roster and I noticed at once I was now finished for the day, and it felt like by divine hand. Then he requested a favour of me and my heart sank. I would not be able to see it in my conscience to deny him an extra shift.

'Nick, I wonder if you would do something for me.' I looked at him expectantly, wondering what I would be committing myself to, but knowing full well my answer would be affirmative. His lifesaving gesture of the job he had presented to me was priceless and beyond earthly value.

'We have a troublesome customer,' he continued. 'Well, he's not so much trouble, more of a bloody nuisance. He's a former army officer, a captain, in fact, been decorated by all accounts, and he's undoubtedly an alcoholic. He makes a constant nuisance of himself, annoying customers by cadging drinks and talking rubbish which gets worse as the evening wears on. Well, the boss gave him a final warning recently and said if he comes in drunk again, he'll ban him. I've got the job of keeping an eye open.' He shifted from one foot to the other and looked uncomfortable and so I decided to come to his rescue. 'You want me to do the night shift?' I suggested with the best smile I could manage.

'Good God, no. Evenings ain't busy here, but I've got a new nighttime barmaid and this is only her second shift, and I need an hour off from six till seven. I wondered if I gave you a description of the captain, whether you would cover for me and keep an eye on him. If he's sober, there's no problem and he's not violent if he's drunk. If necessary, just tell him you have my authority to ask him to leave.' I nodded in agreement and told him he had no need to worry.

'Thanks, Nick, I owe you one,' he said. 'No, you don't,' I replied simply, 'In fact, I owe you, and one day I'll tell you why.'

Bob didn't look surprised.

I slept and dreamt a rerun of my alcoholic hell, and only departed from it when a man in a chef's hat pounded on the door at 5pm and informed me that if I wanted dinner, I should come immediately. I did so and ate alone with thoughts centred on the ramifications of a sober life.

I had the military drunk's description etched in my brain. Smartly dressed, black trilby, black Crombie coat, dark trousers with creases capable of inflicting a knife wound (sic), and shoes you could see to shave in. The new barmaid was a pleasant girl in her early twenties called Mary. Bob explained to her that I was standing in for him for an hour, and then left, opening the pub doors for business as he did so. Mary and I chatted for a while and she confided she had two young children and needed the money to help make ends meet. Then the first customer of the evening arrived. It was the captain, looking exactly as Bob had described him.

I lifted the hatch and left the bar, approached him and asked if he could spare me a couple of minutes. He nodded and then spoke in a typically public school or perhaps military officer's accent.

'Indeed you can, dear boy. I am merely stopping at a tavern on my way to nowhere. Do you think you could manage to purchase me a small brandy?' He smelt like it wouldn't be his first, but I nodded at Mary who obliged and then I carried it to the nearest table with the captain following close behind.

'You're new, my boy,' he sounded inquisitive, eyeing the glass before him as though he was concerned it might be a mirage, and then looked up at me.

'What brings you to the tavern trade, dear boy?' I didn't answer straight away; I found myself on familiar ground and knew he was playing a game, and I wanted to play it to help him.

'Necessity, sir,' I said eventually.

'Who are you? Indeed, what are you?' He persisted.

Only someone who had trodden the same road would understand the complexities of the psyche behind his question, and so I decided to take the bull by the horns. I looked down at the carpeted floor and imagined it was the dusty bare boards of Dr Weiser's surgery, complete with two carrier bags. Then I looked at the captain and our eyes met.

'I am like you, sir,' I said calmly.

'Ex-army?' he enquired.

'No... I'm a drunk!'

He held my gaze, and it lasted half a minute before he responded, and when he did, it was not exactly as I had expected.

'Do you think we were destined to meet?' he asked in a whisper. I didn't tell him I had been wondering the same thing. Instead, I asked him a question.

'Would you like me to help you?'

'I think I am beyond help,' was his reply.

One of the case history-type parables I had written about previously concerned an old soldier who had fought his way across Europe during WWII and survived only to be beaten by the bottle. I told it to him from memory and ended with the words, 'He was buried upright to save space in a pauper's grave, and there was no rest for him even in death. He had died in pain on the alcohol battlefield.'

Suddenly, I was aware that tears were streaming down the captain's face and I knew there was nothing I could do; they had to run their course. They did so for a considerable time as if he wanted to wash away the poison from his brain. Then he took a smartly pressed white linen handkerchief from his breast jacket pocket and ruined its immaculate shape in an effort to restore his calm.

'I was going to an AA meeting, but came here instead.' His voice was a whisper. He looked at his watch, then spoke with a shade more confidence.

'There is still time. I think I will go. Would you come with me?'

'Yes, of course I will,' I replied.

Was I about to become the first barman in history to serve sobriety to a committed drinker? I will never know the answer to that. However, I do know I did my one and only alcohol detox whilst employed as a barman.

19: TIME FLIES

Sobriety transpired to be a whirlwind of events and revelations. I spent my spare time sorting the two carrier bags containing four years of research and study and destroying illegible and many repeats that seemed to exist. I was surprised to find the Doc had written some notes in red ballpoint pen with comments such as, 'Develop this' and 'Excellent observation' and it seemed he was particularly impressed by a lengthy piece describing, 'Alcohol the Anaesthetic'.

I was particularly taken by what I had written on this issue, mainly because I had no recollection of writing it. I consoled myself in the knowledge this applied to a great deal of my written work. Sober, I began to realise the significance of this particular observation. I had reasoned that psychological maturity amongst those who consumed alcohol daily was stunted, in the way smoking is said to do with growth. As I progressed down abstinence street, I realised all my new friends were younger than I was. I also discovered those who were my age seemed to me to be much older, and I was less likely to form social friendships with them. The impact of this realisation really struck home.

I construed in one set of notes that I weighed in at around eight stone (112 lbs) and although I began gaining weight with the introduction of regular meals, a glance in the mirror revealed me as much younger than my years, not hindered by the full head of long, thick hair that the vagrant's life incorporated. A sober world was indeed a very strange place.

I was sad when I moved on from the Barley Mow, but another sober revelation was me being full of ideas (many naïve due to lack of maturity) and equally full of ambition. I also became aware the world was wider than the perspective of the drinker, and full of opportunities that did not exist in the bottom of a glass. Or in the lives of those filling them up for a living.

I felt like I had been born again or, more rationally, into my early twenties, which came with a minor problem… I was actually thirty-two. My aspirations of being a decade younger were aided by appearing to others as being much younger for the reasons stated, and amusingly some put it down to pickling by alcohol. I had already seen my age as a barrier, preventing the advancement of my musical career. Having realised I could easily knock a few years off, I took another look at what I might do.

One agent friend who had not given up on me suggested I could do quite well if I looked at cruising the seven seas and suggested a vocal comedy double act. Word got around of my search, and I received a telephone call from June Collins, an agent of note, who had a famous son called Phil. She suggested I should take a look at a female singer, dancer, and comedienne on her books who she named as Lesley Roach. She was indeed an impressive professional, and we began rehearsing together to see if there was any common ground.

During the first week, Lesley dropped a bombshell – her mother had recently died aged forty-eight as a chronic alcoholic. She described in detail her life with a drunken mother, none of which was a surprise to me but just the same I was stopped dead in my tracks. Lesley was twenty-one and had been at stage school since the age of three, and had therefore been cocooned in a protective bubble. The contrast of her mother's decline had been a monumental experience and here I was, less than six months from being an alcoholic vagrant, thinking of going into business with her. No doubt she would head off into the sunset the very moment I told her of my life.

I decided I would tell Lesley at the rehearsal rooms as soon as we met the next day. I hardly slept the night before my grand reveal, and reminded myself over and over of the commitment I felt to leave alcohol behind me forever. Perhaps this was a test, I told myself; maybe it was exactly what I needed. Responsibility was not something I was familiar with due to the nature of the beast which had lived in me for too long.

I took some of my typed notes with me that read impressively and which had begun life in carrier bags, then sat Lesley down in a side room and asked her if she would please read them while I took a stroll.

I had already chosen a spot to sit where I could see her through several glass partitions, and she was unlikely to see me. When she appeared to be finished, I returned to where she sat.

'Bit too late for my mum, I'm afraid, Nick,' she said wistfully and I nodded. 'It's not too late for you though, Lesley… you see… I'm an alcoholic!'

'I guessed there was some reason why you didn't drink when everyone else did.' She looked calm and then added, 'When do you plan to have your next drink, Nick?'

'Never,' I replied instantly.

'Nothing to worry about then, is there?' was her reply.

Rehearsals went well. We did several practice-type bookings along the way to get some sort of audience reaction, and to get a feel for our own capabilities, something only a fellow pro would understand.

The double act skill was completely new to me, but Lesley adapted much more easily thanks to her stage schooling, to say nothing of West End theatre experience. Then, one day, I was brought down to earth with a bang.

I decided to telephone half a dozen agents to check out their responses to a new comedy, vocal double act. Their reactions were united as one.

'We don't take on cabaret double acts until they have been together for at least five years.'

I was shocked, to say the least, and having broken the news to Lesley, we sat for an age in complete silence, and then abruptly I had a thought.

'Have you heard of the Northern Club Circuit?'

She shook her head.

'They're a mixture of Working Men's Clubs, Social Club establishments and the odd top cabaret venue. There are hundreds in the North of England. Most of it may not sound too sophisticated, but the standard is very high and they've had the very best of entertainment thrown at them for generations. It would mean a lot of travelling, but I've worked the circuit in the past and I know what is required.'

She paused briefly and then spoke with confidence, 'I'm up for it if you are.'

I began contacting northern agents at once, but in an odd twist, Johnny Laycock – a well-known London agent – heard about us from another act and gave us a booking in South London. We went well and the floodgates opened in the south. Within a year, word had spread northwards, and we received our first contract run from a North East agent opening in Middlesbrough in May 1979. Lesley and I went on to do 1,076 performances, between 1977 and 1986, with countless adventures in between.

*

In 1977, Lesley and I had moved to Hounslow and set up home together. Having done so, we signed on at a general practice in nearby Harlington and met the lovely Dr Sutton who became our GP. He was the nicest of men and treated us as if we were his own family. He was fascinated by my stories of life on the streets, and we spent many an evening dining with him at his large olde-worlde home which doubled as a surgery. On one such night, he asked if he could see some of my carrier bag notes, which I duly provided, and a week later he rang me.

'I have a patient who is an Air Stewardess (as they were then known) with British Airways, and she is facing dismissal due to her drinking… unless I can find treatment for her. I wondered if you could help, and before you suggest it, we've been down the detox and AA routes many times.'

I met Lena a week later and knew instinctively – the moment I met her – that I had my hands full. This was a new alcohol package for me; she liked being drunk and determined she was being normal. It was everyone else who had a problem. She certainly needed a detox and could not understand why she couldn't have one every few weeks in order to solve her addiction problem. Then I had an idea.

'What medication are you prepared to make available?' I asked Dr Sutton, unsure what his reaction would be. His reply surprised me.

'What do you want…? Remember, I've read about Dr Weiser, and the story of Ginger,' he added quickly.

'To be safe, I would want to administer 40 x 5mg Chlordiazepoxide capsules four times daily, reducing by 20mg daily. If you've done the maths, you will already know that ends on day ten. She stays at my house with Lesley and me for the duration.' I was emphatic.

'Leave it to me,' was all he said.

Lena was no trouble at all. In fact, she was almost sensible. She arrived as arranged, tottering on 4-inch heels, smelling as I imagined a gin factory to smell and sat down to a hearty dinner. I'd had a case conference of sorts with Dr Sutton the previous afternoon, when he instilled in me, should anything go wrong, to say I was acting on his instructions and my role was simply as an RA. I asked him what he meant by *go wrong*. He simply shrugged, leaving my imagination to contemplate the possibility of having my first death, and I said so out loud.

Far from there being an emergency, the whole procedure went as smoothly as can be, although we did have one sleepless night when all three of us sat up together talking. One happy memory was a grand finale to the exercise. A year later, we attended a celebration dinner at the Heathrow Hotel, where we joined Lena and her BA staff friends to mark her first year alcohol-free. She kept her job and was promoted in the sober years that followed.

It certainly wasn't the end of the matter. Subsequently, I received a modest donation from British Airways and registered the Lansdowne House Alcohol Advisory Unit, which was granted charitable status.

*

Alcoholism is not a fashionable cause, and despite charitable status, I found myself financing it solely through my work with Lesley on the club circuit. The main problem with this rested on my absence from the project in order to earn money, and it meant employing Team Leaders to work in my place. The wages were not good, although I paid them as well as I was able, and their commitment was not as keen as it might have been, had they once suffered at the hands of the bottle. I decided, therefore, that identification with alcohol addiction was essential, and it gave me another idea.

My carrier bag studies were taking shape as a recovery programme, and I decided to select interested and suitable patients who had recovered as a result of it, and train them to use the format as I did. Naturally, the basic and necessary vocational aspect would feature strongly as a result of their personal suffering; by implementing this policy, the foundations for the future were already in place. The fact they had recovered themselves through this teaching had provided their basic training, and all that remained for me to do was to present the infrastructure.

The Unit soon outgrew the patient facilities provided by the kind Dr Sutton, and I decided to talk my problem through with Dr David Marjot, who was the Consultant in charge of the alcoholism and drug dependence unit of the North West Thames Regional Health Authority. I had first met him in 1977, shortly after detoxing Lena for Dr Sutton, and he had recently taken over from the eminent Dr Max Glatt. At the time, he invited me to call on him should I ever need help with my work, and I had done so regularly when needing beds for detox patients. It was a sunny autumn morning when I telephoned him and described my patient level dilemma, and he invited me to join him for lunch the following day to discuss the problem.

The outcome was extraordinary. He listened intently and then observed that if my patient accommodation factor was solved, I wouldn't have a problem and neither would he with his own current long waiting list. I got the message, and following a pleasant lunch and an interesting chat, he departed with the pledge that he would investigate the possibilities of a short lease on empty hospital properties. These had apparently become vacant due to new government care in the community regulations. Two days later, I received a call from Dr Marjot inviting me to attend a meeting with the hospital's Unit General Manager, regarding a vacant detached ward at what he described as the West Gate.

The UGM was Tom McCluskey, a dour Scot and a delightful and forward-thinking hospital executive. The road I was about to take would be rocky, but the following day I became the proud possessor of a two-year lease on the Chaucer Ward (prior to its demolition). Conversion work on it began at once.

It should not be overlooked that Chaucer Clinic would not have got to first base had it not been for the influence of Dr Marjot, following my appeal for help and our subsequent lunch date. We had hit it off immediately, and for me it was a revelation to be working with a man of medicine who really did know about alcohol addiction. His skills encompassed all aspects of substance addiction, including illegal substances, and I remember him confirming my beliefs that legal and illegal drugs required different treatment mindsets. This like-minded discovery encouraged me to dig more deeply into the mind of the great man, and our chats confirmed many of my own theories. As a result, they gave me more confidence in my own abilities.

David Marjot was a Surgeon Commander and Consultant Psychiatrist in the Royal Navy, who then went on to become Advisor in Psychiatry to the Medical Director General of the Royal Navy. Through his various roles, he came to recognise the serious effect alcohol was having on many of the naval personnel and their families. Then, during a workplace conversation, it emerged that a certain Admiral Twiss was also concerned about alcohol consumption but from a perspective of discipline and efficiency.

David, as I now knew him, collected his findings and alerted the senior naval doctor on the Admiral's general staff on how detrimental alcohol was proving. His work was subsequently brought to the attention of Admiral Twiss and he was invited to meet up with him.

Several more meetings followed, during which David pointed out alcohol had become a major element in the personnel problems affecting the service. While he was seeing alcohol casualties in both servicemen and families, there were other issues which contributed to alcohol abuse as service life can be stressful. It was David's hope the Admiral would recognise more needed to be done for *all* concerned, and the age-old rum ration was only part of the alcohol problem. He felt strongly there needed to be a much wider review of the Navy's man-management policy and this needed to be addressed as a matter of urgency.

David was convinced he had made his overall points clear, however, when Twiss was promoted to Head of the Navy, he abolished the navy's rum ration, soon after David's report was published. Sadly, for David and the families that would have benefited, the remainder of his recommendations were not implemented. I was proud to have David as my mentor.

*

There were many other parts to the puzzle I was assembling, not least the emergence of my carrier bag notes which were now in a progressive stage of advancement and in constant use. We often referred to them as the 'ANSWERS' – for want of a better name – and they become the very essence of patients' recovery. All the same, it is hard to imagine how the Chaucer Clinic revolution could have taken place without vision and support. These came in abundance from Abdy Richardson (Chairman of the District Health Authority), Eddie Kane (Chief Executive), and Barclays Bank Manager Jeffroy Rogers, Hounslow, Hayes and Ealing, circa 1977/89. Abdy brought influence, Eddie waved magic wands, and Jeff was a stalwart of the old banking system. He made it work for me overall, but especially in the early years of my post-drinking life. I have fond memories of him and he is in my thoughts often.

One person's forever presence reigned supremely throughout the Chaucer Clinic, Gainsborough, and the current years, and he must be given a special mention. Peter de Villiers fulfilled so many roles I doubt even he could accurately recall all of them, and never was the expression, *'without whom'* more appropriate.

Meanwhile, life moved fast at my new project. I still desperately needed an administrator, and surprisingly a young keyboard player Lesley and I had worked with in cabaret came to the rescue. In Teresa Weiler, we also discovered – by default – a master class organiser, and more importantly she wanted to join us. All I needed now was a right-hand man on the treatment side, and when I found one, it was a woman.

When Nikki de Villiers arrived as a patient, we had just been awarded the Chaucer Ward which we soon discovered had been used for sick geriatric patients. To describe it as a complete mess was a gross understatement, and the first task was a clean-up job – the hardest part of which was ridding the place of the smell of urine. Nikki was a complex patient, although I was not immediately aware of the reasons why, and I had decided to take one step at a time. She told me she was useless at absolutely everything except cleaning and, at this, she would be the best I would ever find. I obliged by giving her the job as Head Cleaner. On the day, it would have been hard to imagine her as a future Assistant Director, but such were her skills, hidden by the evils of alcohol abuse, this would become a reality. Nikki's rise to prominence was meteoric. The change that came about following her last drink was staggering, and although there was much uneven ground along the way, she responded magnificently.

The Chaucer Ward became the Chaucer Clinic and, at its height, was the UK's largest residential alcohol treatment centre with seventy beds, although this did not last long due to residential rules and regulations. There were, in fact, two Chaucers as a result of us outgrowing the first premise prior to its demolition, and we relocated to a much larger building a few hundred yards to the east. Never in my wildest dream could I have imagined the media reaction to my new endeavour, and this all began because the roof of the new building had been seriously damaged by fire. Transfer of the licence was refused until it had been repaired.

I rang up my friend Pete Townshend of *The Who* fame and described the roofing problem, and he immediately sent a cheque to cover the costs of materials; this left me with the minor task of finding skilled labour to do the job. I was deep in thought on the subject, while out with Nikki collecting patient's medication in my car, when I spotted a large group of street drinkers in a nearby park. Suddenly, I had another idea. I braked abruptly and reversed into a parking place and pointed out the forlorn-looking group to her.

'I wonder how many of them are unemployed builders?' I asked her. She looked at me, then at the sinister and filthy-looking rabble, back at me, and then at the rabble again.

'You're not seriously considering approaching that lot, are you? What sort of roof do you think they are going to build you?'

'C'mon, I'll show you how battles are won and lost!' My voice sounded brave. I was not!

She tried to follow at a distance, but I grabbed her hand and made her walk alongside me. Soon, she reclaimed it and we walked shoulder to shoulder. I counted twenty-three in the group who were gathered under some trees about fifty yards away, and as we walked the sound of drunken violence grew forever closer. We were ten yards away when I spoke in my loudest voice.

'Any of you lot know Mad Fred?' The silence didn't last long.

'D'ya mean Spitalfields Fred?' The voice belonged to a wiry, gnarled man of about sixty, although it's difficult to tell when the streets are on the man.

'Yes, that's him,'

'He's a fucking lunatic,' came back the reply. 'Why do you want to know?'

'I don't want to know,' I answered, 'I just want you to know I used to be one of you!'

Most of them were staring at the muddied grass surface that people sunbathed on in better weather, but the spokesman held my gaze.

'So, what do you want?' He didn't sound angry, just inquisitive.

'My name's Nick Charles and I got sick of living like this.' My hand swept the area to include them. 'So I made a study of alcoholic vagrancy, then got sober and opened a recovery centre for prats like me... and you... a sort of landlocked lifebelt facility to save you from drowning in the fuckin' stuff. I want to know if there are any of you who have any building trade skills. If there are, and you want to rejoin the human race, you can come with me now.' My approach was intentionally rough; I knew this fraternity were not impressed by well-spoken do-gooders and only really took notice of those who communicated in their speak.

'What's in it for us?' Now most of the faces looked up expectantly. It was Nikki's voice that answered.

'A bath, clean clothes, four meals a day, a warm bed, all the tea and coffee you can drink, and a cure if you want it. All you do is work for the Guv, doing what you can.' I glanced sideways and saw she was trembling.

'Who's the bitch, Guv?' This was a new voice from somewhere deep within the group.

'She's going to be your fuckin' mother.' My reply was quick and sharp and I'm not sure where the words came from, only that I was in vagrant mode. Perhaps they were inspired, because sixteen of them followed us back to the clinic.

They cleaned up well enough and cleaned me out of funds, but they fixed the roof brilliantly and I rang up Pete to tell him. He sent another cheque.

*

Meanwhile, my one-time keyboard player, Teresa Weiler, was temping her super-admin skills in Richmond, and fortunately she hated it. Thanks to Pete, I could feed and clothe the first batch of no-hopers and pay her for a month. She looked at the place in horror but rolled up her sleeves and turned two rooms into an office in double-quick time. She also produced an information circular to let all appropriate departments throughout the country know that we were here if they had suitable clients. The place was full in no time at all, and funded thanks to her skills and indefatigable efforts. Not only did she become the closest of friends, she developed into an irreplaceable part of the Clinic infrastructure.

The media had a field day. *'Former dosser builds a clinic from the ashes of a fire,'* was one headline. *'One time vagrant advises government on rough sleeper initiative'* was another and the phone never stopped ringing with requests for me to do radio and TV interviews.

Chaucer Clinic grew in both size and reputation, but sadly any hopes I may have had of developing a united front amongst those offering alcohol treatment elsewhere, would bite the dust. Instead, the opposition, which they transpired to be, adopted a league of ungentlemanly conduct which was hell-bent on Chaucer's destruction.

With the benefit of hindsight, I believe there was a reason behind the hate that lasted throughout its eighteen-year life. To begin with, the complexities of treating the client group were not helped by an acute shortage of funding for all of us. For others struggling to survive, reading in the national press, hearing on the radio, and seeing coverage on television of cheques sent to

Chaucer by international stars such as Pete Townshend, Eric Clapton, Phil Collins, Sir Mick Jagger, Paul Simon and Roger Waters must have hurt. An obsessive nature is essential to become a drunk in the first place. To build an alternative methodology based on how you alone believe the client group should be treated, requires an unimaginable pioneer type commitment. For those who had to compete with a former vagrant attempting to establish a new way, and see his face and hear his voice on TV and radio almost every week for a decade or more, must have been difficult. To then see him in a government advisory role alongside Sir George Young on the *'Rough Sleepers Initiative'* must have been hard. To then witness him become the first person to be honoured by the Queen, *'for services to people with alcohol problems'* – when you may have worked as hard and for as long – must have been intolerable. And the press didn't help either with headlines such as, *'From a cardboard box to Buckingham Palace'*.

Word on the block was they were in fear of my work threatening their jobs, which was untrue as the subsequent years proved. My only aim was to develop a different approach to the treatment of alcoholics. This was designed through the eyes and experiences of a vagrant who had returned in one piece from an alcoholic place worse than hell.

I really don't know how I could have handled it differently. I have learnt to my cost that there is little place for innovation in the NHS, and none whatsoever in the fight against alcoholism. Nevertheless, not a day goes by without me wishing I could have mediated with my detractors, and this lives on to the present day.

*

Chaucer closed in October 2006, a victim of drastic funding changes and the introduction of care in the community, which had ironically presented us with our first empty premise. I heard later that the staff at the local hospital alcohol unit held a party, and if we deserved it, I would like them to know the sheer knowledge of this event was punishment enough.

By the time we closed the doors and handed in the keys, Nikki, Teresa, Lesley, and I had spent tens of thousands of pounds of our own money in an effort to save it, most of which was the equity in our houses and pretty much all of our savings and pensions.

We then relocated to Cambridgeshire in the most bizarre fashion. Winter was approaching and we were in varying stages of financial meltdown, and I am quite sure most of my thinking was irrational. We were having a meeting when I suggested Googling for cheap property in the UK; remaining in London was not an option. Teresa did so and up came Huntingdonshire, Cambridgeshire, and Lincolnshire. As Huntingdonshire was first, we Googled it further and the properties that appeared were in a place called Ramsey. Teresa moved first, Lesley and I next, but Nikki held out for a miracle as only she could, then finally succumbed and joined us ten months later.

Nikki and I tried very hard to set up an Internet treatment project which we called '*Nick and Nikki's Place*' and we wasted a great deal of money we couldn't afford. It had good credentials with 'ANSWERS' but was ill-conceived, not the least due to an attempt to use a video producer who had not the slightest grasp of addiction. The media, with many recollections of successful and newsworthy experiences of us in Chaucer days, were convinced I would make a comeback. I was persuaded to introduce '*Nick and Nikki's Place*' on Sky News; stupidly, I agreed and we made a complete hash of it. All I succeeded in doing was to prove I was hopelessly ill-equipped and nowhere near ready. The saving grace was probably the fact my piece aired on the 5am news with few watching, and this may have saved us much ridicule. However, I had learnt an important lesson. The experience left me with a deep fear and a feeling of doom that my work would now be confined to the press history books, or to use the modern version, Wikipedia.

One day, Teresa – who was now playing a serious part in my endeavours to move forward in my work – rang to ask if I had registered with a doctor and I had not. After a mild chastisement, she suggested picking up both Lesley and me, and taking us to register at what she insisted was the best Practice in Ramsey. We complied. When I was asked for my occupation I quite correctly replied, '*Director of the Gainsborough Foundation*', which Teresa and I had recently registered as a not-for-profit limited company, ready for '*Nick and Nikki's Place*' to trade under. A week later, and suffering from a dose of flu, I met a charming lady doctor who introduced herself as Dr Rita – half of a husband and wife GP partnership. Having offered sympathy, she prescribed some medication and then conversationally enquired about the nature of my work. Still suffering the loss of Chaucer, I didn't feel much like talking about my failures and instead told her to Google nickcharles.co.uk, and all would be explained. The next day I received a call from her doctor partner husband Dr Arun Aggarwal, with a surprising outcome.

'Mr Charles?' were the questioning words spoken on the other end of my landline phone. 'Yes,' I responded casually, not recognising the voice.

'It's Dr Arun from the surgery, you met my wife Dr Rita yesterday; how is your flu?' I responded favourably as I was having a better day, and then he surprised me. 'I have an hour to spare. Could you pop down to the surgery so we could have a chat?' When I arrived, I was made extremely welcome.

In order to reply honestly to his enquiries concerning my plans now that Chaucer was no more, I explained I really hadn't got any, although I was considering looking for premises which might be suitable for a Chaucer replacement. I also described 'ANSWERS' as my treatment programme in waiting.

'I have a more practical suggestion,' he studied my reaction which, although it didn't show, was one of complete surprise. 'How say you present your skills to patients in surgery?' he continued.

Frankly, I was dumbstruck and thoughts cascaded through my head. I remembered how well it had worked with Drs Weiser and Sutton although not with any degree of sophistication, and this would certainly be called for in a modern-day medical centre set-up. Suddenly it *did* seem a practical plan and I decided in an instant I had nothing to lose and said so.

'Right, I'll do a patient referral by giving them your phone number, then we will provide a room for you to meet, and we'll see how it goes from there. Is that okay?' said Dr Arun. It was a no-brainer and I agreed.

The shaping and planning of the service led to an extremely successful partnership which spread to thirty-three other

Practices across the region. It did not happen overnight and, in fact, went through many degrees of change, and there were the inevitable hoops to jump through. The end result was a slick and super service, the like of which had never been seen before.

Dr Arun, it is true to say, fitted neatly and snugly into the time capsule team with Drs Weiser, Sutton, and Marjot (in order of appearance). He brought with him Dr David Roberts – a skilled adviser and Elizabeth Sargent OBE, an authority on social care and emergency care improvement. They all possessed the unique quality of believing in innovation, and all had individual talents which were vital at certain times when we worked together. One quality they all shared in abundance related to alcoholism. It was the courage and foresight to recognise that without innovation, there would never be a way forward to defeat an enemy which had ruled since the beginning of time. And for which there was no medical rule book.

Despite the overwhelming success of the Gainsborough service, it fell victim to politics and a lack of financial support, which can only be described as history repeating itself. Dr Arun Aggarwal, as the innovative Medical Lead for Gainsborough, did everything within his power to save what he saw as a remarkable innovation. He paid tribute to the service as follows.

'Never once, in my thirty years of medicine have I encountered an alcohol treatment programme, as efficient and as magnificently successful as 'ANSWERS' which has had unprecedented successes. This outcome is radically different to others' experiences up and down the country and I have been the envy of my Royal College colleagues nationwide, for several years.'

*

Alcoholism, which ranks alongside the most devastating and complex diseases known to man, and which maims and kills with impunity, continues to be treated by methods that are archaic and the laughing stock of the seriously informed. Someone, somewhere in the world, dies as a direct result of alcohol every ten seconds (WHO).

The seriousness of the worldwide failure to successfully address this disease is epitomised by the mainstay treatment being self-help groups. These are run by the local plumber, bank manager, shopkeeper, builder, road sweeper, etc., in the shape of well-meaning ensembles of recovered victims, purely because they are free. The longer this continues, without recognition of the need for an expertly organised partnership between those with insider alcohol knowledge and medical authorities, the longer the alcohol threat will reign supreme. Suffice it to say, and in the final analysis, the main victims will continue to be, those with alcohol problems and their families.

You couldn't make it up!

EPILOGUE

December 2020.

Having decided to write the story of the 'ANSWERS' odyssey in the shape of '50 Years of Hard Road', I completed the final touches as darkness fell on a December afternoon in 2020. My thoughts wandered to the future, and I was suddenly weighed down by a heavy and despondent heart; now what was I to do?

Born in 1944, I was seventy-six on December 15th 2020 and in that moment, and for the first time in my life, I considered the possibility that my sober alcohol endeavours may never be realised. This despite my faith and belief that my dreadful alcoholic fall from grace and subsequent work in the alcohol field was, in fact, my destiny.

When the BBC filmed a documentary of my life, in 1998, I closed the proceedings with the words, 'The thought of reaching the end of my life, having not achieved what I set out to achieve, is more than I can bear to contemplate.'

My grandfather had died when he was fifty-nine, my father seventy-two, and for the first time ever, I realised I may have run out of time. On December 13th, I had celebrated forty-four years alcohol-free, and the fact I was now in my twilight years had only just occurred to me. I was plummeted into a black abyss which was filled with panic and I rushed into my garden for air.

I sat on a chair designed and intended for summer use and shook uncontrollably and my teeth banged together relentlessly. It was 2° Celsius but my training told me this was not caused by the winter chill, rather a bizarre panic attack and an alarming drop in my body temperature. I rushed back into the house and hugged a radiator for dear life.

Slowly, I regained my composure and prayed to God requesting forgiveness if I was still behind with my payments. I returned to the tiny attic office where alcohol educational dreams were made, peoples' lives were saved, and where recently I had completed the 'ANSWERS' story. I sat facing an empty computer screen.

Instinctively, I pressed the start button and for once remembered my password; the ensuing glow lit up the darkening winter afternoon and almost at once e-mail alerts told me I had two unread messages. My mouth went dry and my hands were trembling.

The first was to confirm a substantial contract from an international publishing company based in the UK, who distributed their titles across Europe, North America, Asia, and Australasia. It could have been the entertainer in me, but I felt there should have been an orchestra in my brain reaching a climax in a symphony. Instead, a silence existed which seemed out of place. With a sense of calm I did not feel, I gripped the sides of my desk for stability and switched my attention to the second email message and forced myself to read the words.

It was from a financial institution which had a philanthropic wing, and they wrote in support of innovative and alternative options in the field of mental health. It went on to say they had been made aware of the British Medical Journal and the Royal College honouring my work and they approved of the aims and objectives. There was also praise for my approach in a society where there was precious little recognition of the symptoms, or understanding of the disease of alcoholism. It ended with a telephone number should I wish to meet with them and discuss the future.

I read both several times, and then turned my attention to the completed manuscript I called '50 Years of Hard Road' that two minutes previously had lacked direction. And I felt overcome by the power of destiny.

I collected my thoughts, responded with an acceptance to my new publisher's offer, and switched my attention to the second communication and picked up the phone.

'Hello, I would like to make an appointment to meet with…'

Definitely not **The End.**

AWARDS AND ACHIEVEMENTS

Member of the British Empire New Year Honours List *(For services to people with alcohol problems).*

Alcohol Programme: *Winners 'Vision Awards' sponsored by Department of Health for Pulse Magazine.*

Alcohol Programme: *Winners 'The British Medical Journal (BMJ) Primary Care Team of the Year Award' sponsored by MDDUS.*

Alcohol Programme: *Winners 'NHS East of England Regional Innovation Fund Award' (RIF).*

Alcohol Programme: *Winners 'Innovative Clinical Care Enterprise Award, Royal College of General Practitioners' (RCGP) sponsored by MDU.*

Alcohol Programme: *Winners 'Six Category Overall Winners Enterprise Award, Royal College of General Practitioners' (RCGP) sponsored by MDU.*

As winners of a £127,500 *NHS Innovation Award*, the treatment programme now called 'ANSWERS' was licensed to the Gainsborough Foundation (GF) as a comprehensive teaching tool. It was used in surgeries and medical centres across two counties for eight years to treat alcohol-dependent patients, and others were trained in the art of delivering it.

Founded the Chaucer Clinic, the UK's largest alcohol rehabilitation project.

Adviser to the government on the Rough Sleepers Initiative with Sir George Young.

Founder of Addiction Network which had 1 million followers and ran for 5 years.

'The Nick Charles Case Book' BBC Radio, which produced the first alcohol case history CD recorded by the BBC.

Designed and founded the 'ANSWERS' Alcohol Recovery Programme, honoured and lauded by the medical profession.

Awarded a partnership contract with 150+ GPs across Cambridgeshire and to work alongside them in medical centres.

Autobiographies: 'Through A Glass Brightly', '50 Years of Hard Road'.

Biography: Nikki de Villiers – 'Life in the Devil's Cellar'.

Biography: Lesley Roach – 'A Brutal Bequest'.

True Life Alcohol Adventure Story: 'Miss Reeves' (For Young People – told through the eyes of the supernatural).